Walking to Freedom through

FREEDOM
WALK
A True Story

By Steve and Noit Hyde

First Printing   *2000 copies*   *January 2020*

Illustrations by Moeun Chansokha.
Portrait of Noit Hyde, by Chris Cox with Souch Photo.
Cover design by Destinyy.

Published By:

Words of Life Ministries
P.O. Box 2581, Phnom Penh, 12306, Cambodia
www.asiaforjesus.org
www.facebook.com/cambodiasteve
steve@asiaforjesus.com

ISBN: 9789996340246
ISBN-13: 978-99963-40-24-6
ISBN issued by the National Library of Cambodia

Printed in the Kingdom of Cambodia.

Endorsements

"When at the age of 16, Noit Hyde escaped from the brutal forces of the communist Khmer Rouge in Cambodia, God displayed His sovereign plan for her life to change the lives of many others through the Gospel. In this new work, Freedom Walk, her husband, Steve Hyde, tells about her horrific experiences that led to her victorious walk with Jesus. Today she and Steve are back in Cambodia ministering to thousands of people. Their work is a testimony to the power of God and the Gospel of Jesus Christ. This book will keep you on the edge of your seat and also on your knees in prayer. I highly recommend it."

Steve Gaines, Ph.D.
Pastor, Bellevue Baptist Church, Memphis, TN
President of the Southern Baptist Convention

*"'**Freedom Walk**' draws you into the dark valley of the Khmer Rouge with all of its atrocities and then leads you out to the bright mountain of love's transformation."*

*"'**Freedom Walk**' is a moving story of deprivation, survival, and tragedy that becomes a testimony to the power of Christ's love. The real revolution in Cambodia was not the Khmer Rouge's social experiment gone awry, but the power of Jesus Christ to transform a shattered life into a thriving testimony of love and forgiveness."*

Andrew Rankin, Ph.D.
Senior Pastor, Freedom Church, Owasso, Oklahoma
Author of "Do Love"

"We all have a story. Our lives are, in fact, a collection of stories — personal narratives that define and give context to our lives. Our stories give readers clues about our existence, frustrations, hopes, and aspirations. If you really want to get to know someone well then listen to their stories. Stories unlock insight and foster understanding.

The stories recorded in this book were forged in the furnace of unimaginable horrors unleashed by a madman on his own people. My dear friend Noit survived those horrors and has kept these stories buried deep in her heart — until now.

The stories in this book will give you tearful insight into the courageous heart of a young woman whose journey has taken her from extreme loss and deep suffering to remarkable purpose. Noit's story is not over. Her continuing story speaks of the healing power of the gospel and the beauty of Jesus. Her story will inspire yours."

Omar C. Garcia
Missions Pastor, Kingsland Baptist Church
Katy, Texas

---

*"**Freedom Walk**" by Steve, Noit and Paul Hyde is a compelling story of courage, hope and goodness that inspires all the best in our humanity even when we are faced with the most despicable and overwhelming circumstances.*

I have been travelling in and out of Cambodia at least annually, since 1992. In that time I have heard many horrifying and horrendous stories from people who survived the Khmer Rouge years. Each story is heart wrenching and speaks of a time that is incomprehensible in its devastation to those involved.

I have personally known Steve and Noit for over ten years now. They are wonderful friends from whom I have learned so much. It is staggering to me that Noit is such a marvellous and amazing person given how she walked, in her own words, from having a "heart that was totally dead" towards anything positive in life into being the life-giving and loving person she is today.

*In a world that offers cruelty, dislocation, bloodshed and despair to so many of our fellow human beings, Noit's story is an inspiration of how someone's personal history can be so dramatically transformed. The message of Jesus, that is, the love, acceptance and hope He offers is so totally captured in Noit's story. I love the Hyde family. I love their authenticity. I love their love for all people. You too will love them and their God by the time you finish "**Freedom Walk**".*

Peter McHugh
Senior Minister, Stairway Church
Melbourne, Australia

"'Freedom Walk' by my friends Steve and Noit Hyde is a must read for anyone wanting to read of how God's grace does what only God's grace can do; leave us in total amazement. They have walked through the darkest moments and yet become the brightest light of love I have ever seen. A week with Steve and Noit in Cambodia gave me an upgrade in radical trust in God."

Leif Hetland
President, Global Mission Awareness
Atlanta, Georgia
Author of *"Giant Slayers"*

"There are very few books that I consider a "page turner". What I mean by that is that you just can not put the book down. Each page is filled with such suspense, action, drama and powerful gripping emotion that you can not wait to read the next page. You get lost in time reading it.

This is such a true "page turner" book. The life story of Noit is both powerful and gripping. It tells of the incredible depth of God's love, mercy, protection and grace. It is also the story of miracles. It is obvious that God had His hand on Noit from birth. She truly is a "chosen one". Her story of survival through both the Vietnam War and the Pol Pot Communist regime of Cambodia is both heartwarming and incredible.

To us in the West it is a story almost beyond belief. Yet, her story is true. There should be a movie made on her life based on this book. It's that good! God chose her and provided for her and is using her to touch the world for Christ. She truly is one of the great and mighty modern day heroes of the faith. Reading this book will capture you from the very first page. It will challenge every reader to deepen his or her own level of commitment to Christ.

This book should be read by every true believer to understand exactly what it truly means to live and walk under the Lordship of Christ."

Dr. Wade Akins
Global Missionary , Author of "Being a 24/7 Christian"
and "Pioneer Evangelism".
www.pioneermissions.org

*"'**Freedom Walk**' is an amazing story of tragedy, trial and triumph! I couldn't stop reading except to wipe my eyes of the tears running down my face. It is a compelling story of one woman's journey from death to life on the wings of grace and God's sovereignty. Through the power of Christ and the release of forgiveness, she would find freedom and pave a way for a nation to discover hope. I recommend this book and the Savior it exalts to every living soul on earth!"*

Randy Howard
Senior Pastor, The Gate Church
Victorville, California

"If you want to read a warm, fuzzy story, this book may not be for you. On the other hand, if you are willing to read the story of a little girl growing to a mature woman through genocide, persecution, hunger, sickness, and hopelessness, this might be a book for you. Warning: it could be helpful to have Kleenex nearby. Steve Hyde's gripping story of his wife, Noit, may have you weeping in sorrow, as you read of her early life, then weeping with joy as she discovers hope through faith in Jesus Christ and overcomes her past with a glorious present, and a promising future."

Dr. Dan Crawford
Senior Professor of Evangelism & Missions; Chair of Prayer, Emeritus
Southwestern Baptist Theological Seminary
Fort Worth, Texas

"My wife Jean and I have been moved beyond words by Noit, Steve, and Paul's testimony recorded in this book. The retelling of this period of the history of Cambodia captures the experiences of Noit in such a way that brings the reader into a depth of understanding of what the people endured at the hands of a wicked despot. It brings deeper appreciation of the grace of God and His healing power in the life of a soul surrendered to the Lordship of Christ Jesus.

The Body of Christ owes a debt of gratitude to Noit for her faithfulness in consistently returning good for evil. Also for the Freedom Walk undertaken by Steve and Paul in order to commemorate the horrendous experiences endured by Noit and countless others. One can't help but appreciate Steve and Noit's Gospel-centered ministry born out of such adversity. Our Lord does indeed give "beauty for ashes, and the oil of joy for mourning ".

Having served in the expansive vineyard God has given Steve and Noit, both in Cambodia and the Philippines, as well as spending quality personal time with them, we can attest that Steve , Noit, and their family are indeed "the real deal". In a time and place that many of us serve Christ from a place of comfort and convenience, it is both challenging and convicting to read of the sacrifices they continually make to make Christ known.

Our prayer is that our Lord would be pleased to use this book, a true labor of love, to make the Name and the fame of Jesus known. As the Scriptures plainly say, He "will be exalted among the nations, (He) will be exalted in the earth!" Psalm 46:10"

Craig and Jean Stockdale
Bible teachers, Authors, and Missionaries
Standing Near the Cross, Inc.
Memphis, Tennessee

"Few of us will ever have a front row seat to genocide, slavery, escape, survival and the struggle to build any sort of hope in life. Most of us wouldn't want to experience those sorts of challenges firsthand. Yet there is tremendous encouragement to be found from someone who has seen the worst of this world and eventually come to see the best. Noit Hyde is one of those people and this is story.

Written masterfully by her husband Steve, **Freedom Walk** *is a stunning, true biography of Noit's journey from death to life. It's also the story of how Jesus' love is still the most revolutionary, healing, life-changing source of hope the world has ever seen.* **Freedom Walk** *is a walk we all need to take, allowing God to make sense of our past and guide us into a life-giving future. My dear friends, Steve and Noit, have given their entire lives to see that others have the opportunity to take their own walks toward freedom in a relationship with Jesus.*

So, sit down. Open your heart. Then open Freedom Walk. After that, I guarantee you'll never be the same."

Ron Merrell
Teaching Pastor
Heights Church
Prescott, Arizona

Freedom Walk

Walking to Freedom through the
Killing Fields of Cambodia

❧   *A True Story* ⟩

Table of Contents

Freedom Walk

Dedication

To Noit, an amazing wife, wonderful mother and partner bringing the Gospel of Restoration to the lives of so many children.

Your love is unmatched on this earth and your compassion has no limits. No one could imagine by meeting you the hell that you survived and how Jesus though His grace, has turned the worst nightmare into dreams come true for hundreds and thousands of your Cambodian children.

To the surviving victims of the Khmer Rouge. I pray you find peace in your heart. We will not forget you. The tragedy of Noit's life mirrors so many survivors in Cambodia and I pray you can find the same peace she has.

Acknowledgements

A special thanks to my Mom, Lyn Hyde, for helping to proofread the book so that this book "Freedom Walk" would become a reality.

I appreciate all others who gave me proofreading help and editing suggestions especially Dr. Andrew Rankin and Craig Petty for their helpful editorial feedback.

I am also grateful for Pastor Sokha illustrating the book "Freedom Walk" so that Noit's story could be clearly depicted through pictures. Being a survivor of the Khmer Rouge himself certainly brought accuracy to the illustrations, but also reminded him of the pain of the past. Thank you for your sacrifice so that future generations may know the horror of what really happened to the Cambodian people.

Preface

They shot my father for being a teacher
And dumped his body in a field.
They enslaved my family
And forced us to toil for their schemes,
torturing us to death.
They starved us
And I watched my family die.
They threatened horrible death on us
If we shed a tear as our family died.
We were once a large happy family
Now we are two.

To be a survivor of genocide
All you had to do was not die.
Yet, many survivors still die every day
In their hearts.
Many survivors live in tormented trauma
Not visible on the outside.
Many survivors are still haunted by demons in the night
And scream when no one can hear them.
Many survivors still live each day in fear
Numbing their senses and their hearts.
Many survivors wish they had died
And have no hope for tomorrow.
Some survivors walk an arduous journey
And eventually find freedom.

This is one such story
From Cambodia's Killing Fields.

Freedom Walk

Part One: A Journey to Hell

Just the name of the country, "Cambodia", evokes ideas of an exotic oriental land and images of jungles with quaint thatched houses. For some it triggers images of ancient civilizations forgotten to time and buried under dense jungles, while for others who only know of its modern history recall the words "Killing Fields" which are etched into their minds. Some emotions conjured up involved adventure, some fear and others curiosity of this little known country.

In its zenith, nearly half a millennium before Christopher Columbus ever found his way to the Americas, Cambodia was once one of the most powerful and modern kingdoms of the world. Its cities and temples were crafted out of stone and still remain as archeological splendors over a thousand years later. The Cambodian empire started being formed with a warrior queen around AD 60. The people would emerge out of the jungle and begin building cities and fortresses. By AD 802 they had become a powerful kingdom and declared their independence from all other kingdoms. The boundary of this kingdom stretched across what is today modern Cambodia, Vietnam, Laos, Thailand and even parts of Malaysia.

Through the centuries, kings ruled and fought. Sometimes it was with other nations, and other times it was with other members of the monarchy who sought to overthrow the current king. There were periods of war and brief periods of peace. However, because of the geography of Cambodia they were significantly isolated. There were no seaports to link Cambodia to the world and no easy ways to access Cambodia through neighboring countries. Only a long and difficult journey over three hundred miles up the Mekong River and its tributaries would allow access to this hidden, yet powerful kingdom.

During the Angkor Kingdom they built massive monuments, palaces and cities which still remain today. Their Angkor Kingdom fell in AD 1431 to the rising Thailand invaders. They built astonishing monuments such as Angkor Wat, which many regard as one of the largest religious buildings in the world today.

Over the nation's 2000 year history they have experienced many interactions with foreign powers. Some positive, some negative. They adopted Hinduism from southern India, though retained their own animistic practices. As Thailand grew in influence they often considered the up-and-coming nation "cousins", and adopted many similar Buddhist practices, yet still retained their other roots. They adapted their writing system and grammar from ancient Sanskrit, yet today they proudly value their modern Khmer language. They were dominated by the French for nearly a hundred years, and many medical and technical words today are clearly rooted in French.

In the 16th century the first Christians came to Cambodia, first from the Catholic Portuguese and then with the Protestant Dutch. Throughout the next five hundred years the Christian church would grow slightly and then be smashed. Yet the church would never completely die, no matter how harshly it was persecuted. The teachings and practice of this small church have seemed to always clash with the Cambodian empire and its hierarchical social structure.

During the French colonial control from AD 1863-1954 Vietnamese immigration grew and remains a significant issue today bringing a mixture of Vietnamese and Chinese domination into urban areas, especially in business.

In the modern era, since Cambodian independence from France, the nation has experienced significant social and political conflict. The independence was ushered through war and violence, those vying for power wanting to take total control of the nation and its resources. At times, the leaders have leaned toward Soviet style communism, then to the counter influence of the rising democratic American power. Currently the nation is leaning toward Maoist-style neo-socialism. All of these foreign influences have left lasting effects on the nation today, but the core is still uniquely Cambodian and outside influence has become mixed with indigenous Cambodian practices.

In 1975 the American-backed government of Cambodia finally fell to the Maoist-backed guerilla forces which were known to the world as "Khmer Rouge" or Red Cambodians. The Khmer Rouge would lead the nation to a path which would nearly destroy itself. It was during this political and social conflict that this story is set. Few knew it, but the conflicts that were happening were leading to one of the world's worst genocides and near extinction of the Cambodian nation.

Millions would die as ruthless leaders decimated their own country and tortured and killed their very own citizens.

But, amongst incredible horror and anguish a young woman walked a path out of genocide and into freedom.

Sometime in the rainy season between 1962 and 1964 a baby girl was born to a loving mother in a hospital in Phnom Penh, Cambodia. This little girl was born as child number six, to Hieng Hun. The pregnancy was difficult and the labor more difficult than normal for a sixth child. When she was born she was frail and small. The doctors told the mother to just throw her away because she likely wouldn't live. They reasoned that to let her die from exposure in a Buddhist temple was better than to care for this weak baby girl. In so doing, they reasoned that as the baby died of exposure, the proximity to the Buddha would lessen the negative karma. Hieng looked at the tiny little baby and she was filled with love and hope. The callousness of the doctors shocked her as a young Buddhist mother. Hieng, with her mother's guidance, took her little child home, not expecting her to live, but just hoping to keep her alive for a few more days. Somehow, though, the little girl survived day after day and week after week. So, Hieng decided to give child number six a name. Hoping for some good luck they named her "Nimol" which means "perfect". Her family never used that name though, they called her by a nickname "Noit", just because it sounded cute.

Her difficult survival from birth would mark her life. Her country was already engaged in civil war. Politically, the iron hand of Prince Norodom Sihanouk crushed any opposition. Those who persisted to oppose his autocratic control on power either disappeared or joined a jungle rebellion. This rebellion was derogatorily named by Sihanouk the "Khmer Rouge" or "Red Khmers" because of their Maoist and Leninist persuasion. Sihanouk was also a strong socialist, though ironically, a monarch. Royalty, by principle, directly opposed the goal of communism to destroy the *bourgeoisie*, or elite social class, in society to make everyone "equal" by creating a *proletariat* which would be devoid of any social classes.

In the 1960's, communism was sweeping the world. This ideology promised prosperity and equality to everyone but having been untested over time faced little opposition from local communities. Western nations, led by America, were heavily engaged with a fight to preserve the last democratic nation in Indochina, South Vietnam. Sihanouk had allowed the North Vietnamese to use Cambodia as a sanctuary and operated the fabled Ho Chi Minh Trail. Cambodia was no longer neutral in the eyes of the west. Therefore, the CIA engineered an overthrow of Sihanouk by paying off one of his corrupted generals, Lon Nol. In early 1970 as Sihanouk was visiting Moscow to tout his socialist progress, he was overthrown militarily and legislatively. Soon there after as the American puppet came to power, the US began extensive bombing of the Ho Chi Minh Trail to obliterate the North Vietnamese supply lines.

Unwilling to accept exile from his country Sihanouk began fighting for his own survival and the survival of the nearly two thousand year old monarchy by joining the very jungle rebellion which was stranded by his advisories. Through his recruitment thousands of additional young troops were added to the ranks. The rebellion he joined, the Khmer Rouge, was actually made up of his political enemies who had been oppressed by him. They were able to convince him that all the hurt of the past was forgiven, but in reality they were using him for his recruiting abilities. Once they accomplished their military objectives they quickly disregarded their old nemesis Sihanouk.

During these years, the Vietnam War between the Americans and North Vietnamese was also in full swing. Noit's family lived around Phnom Penh, a mere 120 kilometers (75 miles) from the South Vietnamese border and less than 150 miles from the heart of Saigon. The Cambodian civil war gradually became an international war and the skies were filled with thousands of B-52 bombers carpet bombing Cambodia daily. Noit's childhood was not playful, but fearful. She feared the bombings, she feared that at any moment she could be killed.

One day, after playing with her cousins while visiting her uncle in *Ta Khmao*, a southern suburb of Phnom Penh, she laid down at noon to rest inside their traditional wood house. Though it was hot outside, she decided to shut the wooden shutters to block the sunlight so she could rest. The sticky tropical weather saps anyone's strength so resting for a few hours during the peak of the noon hours when the sun is at its hottest is the normal practice. Suddenly, she was awakened by a horrible explosion which shook the entire house. A B-52 had dropped its full load of nearly a hundred bombs on the small suburb. It was as if the fires of hell had been unleashed on them. Shrapnel peppered the entire side of the house. In panic and fear those in the room gripped each other tightly not knowing if the next blast would rip them to pieces.

Eventually, the rumble grew silent and the only sound was the whimpering of children. Once they felt safe, they exited the house to inspect the damage. Trees had been blown apart with branches littering the ground. Houses lay in rubble. The survivors crowded together trying to make sense of what just happened and why. Why were resting families a military target? Who attacked them? Who dropped the bombs? There was so much confusion and panic.

Upon inspecting the damage to their house, they found that the shrapnel did not penetrate the window shutters because they were made of Cambodian hardwoods. If she had left the wood shutters open, her little body would have been ripped to pieces. Times would come when she would reflect on that day and wish that she had died. Yet, once again, at only a young age she escaped the clutches of death.

The ongoing war, bombings and fear would only intensify into a hopelessness. Clearly the bombings were only bringing more pain to the people. The government was losing control of the country village by village each day. The Khmer Rouge were capitalizing on the fear and destruction delivered by the American bombers and turned it into a recruiting mechanism. Thousands of young people, fearing the wrath of the Khmer Rouge or occupation by foreign armies, joined its ranks in an effort of self-preservation.

Just at the crack of dawn, early one morning Noit woke to the sound of small arms fire and the beating sound of helicopter blades. It was only 6:00am, but the normally clear skies were full of activity. A C-130 was circling and wave after wave of helicopters flew toward the US Embassy. It was only days earlier that the US Ambassador had promised that America would never abandon its partners. That day was April 12, 1975. It was the day that everyone lost hope. By 11:00am nearly 4,000 military advisers, diplomats and Cambodian government officials who had been loyal to the Americans were gone. Only the acting Prime Minister was left with a small staff who were uninformed as to the evacuation. Each subsequent day, the sounds of war would grow stronger and stronger.

The following Thursday morning, as the sun quickly grew hot in its intensity, the war came right into Noit's house, the last place where there was any safety. On the morning of April 17, 1975, she and her family would descend into hell itself as the Khmer Rouge victoriously marched into Phnom Penh. The American backed troops had been defeated and the last remaining soldiers were stripping off their uniforms and discarding any identification in order to shrink into the traumatized population. Phnom Penh had been surrounded for months and the city was only surviving by the emergency rations airlifted in. Their would be no place to run too. The only hope would be to be to blend into the massive crowds of traumatized citizens.

All the urban inhabitants of Phnom Penh were identified by the number "17" and unknown to them, marked for death. At the time, Noit had nearly fifty immediate relatives, including parents, grandparents, aunts, uncles, cousins, nieces and nephews.

Chapter 3

The Day the Bombs Went Silent

Thursday, April 17, 1975 would be a day that the people of Phnom Penh would not forget. For years there had been the constant sounds of war reverberating in the air. In recent days the war had come so close that the sounds of war surrounded the entire capital city. Mortar attacks were a daily occurrence as Phnom Penh had been under siege for more than two years and was supplied only by air and a few boats navigating the treacherous waters of the Mekong River from Vietnam. Now the mortar attacks grew closer and included blasts from grenades with the sporadic sound of small arms fire. The beautiful French-designed city with its wide boulevards and grandiose architecture was once referred to as the "Pearl of Indochina", but now its previous population had swelled threefold to more than three million people.

As Noit and her family woke early on the 17th the city was eerily quiet. For once it seemed you could even hear the sounds of birds chirping. There was something missing in the deafening quiet. The sound of war was gone: no rockets exploding, bombs dropping and no rat-tat-tat of machine gun fire. Just silence.

Noit quickly had a shower and ate a little left over rice from the day before. The remaining little tin of sardines which had been airlifted in was the meals' sustenance. As she ate, there was an expectation of peace, but also a nervousness. Never mind the complexities of the situation and the fact that no one knew anything about these secretive black clad soldiers that they only knew as "Red Khmer". No one even knew who the leaders were. It was assumed that King Sihanouk had taken over the leadership of the Khmer Rouge, therefore, to welcome them would presumably return the country to a more peaceful time before his expulsion.

The mysterious enemy which had previously been out of sight was now entering the city unopposed. Though the Khmer Rouge were ethnically identical in their complexion and language, their appearance was unique. Most of these soldiers were teenagers, brandishing all sorts of weapons both big and small. Some had M-16's which were confiscated from US-backed Lon Nol troops while others had the classic communist insurgent AK-47 rifles and Chinese-made B-40 rocket launchers. These expressionless soldiers were all wearing well-worn black clothes with the occasional red *karma* scarf draped around their neck. They walked through the city with little apparent direction. The populace nervously welcomed them, hoping the war would be over and their lives could return to normal. Few knew, or cared, about the politics of the various armies. They only hoped that whoever took power would leave them alone to resume their lives, to live in peace with the possibility at self-improvement through a normal livelihood.

The young occupiers commandeered abandoned US military jeeps and started moving through the city blaring an announcement:

"Attention: The Americans are going to bomb the city! All residents need to temporarily leave the city for a few days for safety while we secure the capital. There is no need to lock your doors or take belongings because we will protect everything. Everyone must move immediately for your safety!"

Everyone was scared. Noit, having previously survived B-52 bombing raids and artillery bombardments, was especially scared. Scared for an unknown future, but also scared of the random devastation of B-52's. Her father had been separated from the family so Noit, her siblings and her mother tried to go where they thought he was. The indomitable Khmer Rouge soldiers blocked her way though. She needed to go south to get to her father, but the Khmer Rouge soldiers would only let them go east on highway number 1, toward Saigon, Vietnam. She didn't know it then, but she would never see her father again and would only learn of his fate many years later.

Having been blocked from going to find their father, Noit's family decided to stay with as many relatives as they could. At least in the uncertainty of the day they could be with those they loved and trusted. Though they were told not to take any belongings, they didn't want to leave anything important behind. They gathered their important documents, money, jewelry, clothes, family pictures, possessions, including motorcycles and even their uncle's car and in a band of about fifty people started to head out of the city. One precious belonging was Noit's uncle's convertible car. There was no gas for the vehicle, but they decided to pile the belongings inside and push it along the road because it was too valuable to leave behind.

The way was clogged with people so that no one could ride a vehicle or barely even walk forward. Three million people all converged on three or four roads at the same time. Noit's family pushed their car, inch by inch, not mile by mile. The Khmer Rouge had shut down almost every road out of the city, but the people were being directed to specific areas. The entire population of more than three million people were all moving at once. As they were leaving they began to have premonitions that all would not be as peaceful as they had hoped for. Those who argued with the stoic communist soldiers or tried to resist were hauled away or shot on the spot. Even the sick and elderly were forced to move. Some people were being carried on stretchers with intravenous tubes attached to their arms with bottles of fluids being held over their bodies. There was no allowance for compassion. Patients were walking down the road still connected to IV bottles being held aloft by a stick, or the bedridden being pushed on wheeled hospital beds down the boulevards.

These survivors from Phnom Penh felt that they were lucky to survive, but in effect they had been deemed expendable enemies of the state. They would be considered worthless and told, "For you to live is of no value, and to die is no loss." They would follow up the masochistic phrase with another equally demonic saying, "at least your blood will make the ground softer".

Most of those branded "17" would be lost forever. Their bodies discarded across the nation in rural fields, jungle swamps or unmarked mass graves. As Noit left the city, she held hope that she would only be gone for a few days, but the future was completely uncertain. Fear soon enveloped her.

Life previous to the Khmer Rouge take over in 1975 was not so good either. The entire region was embroiled in the Vietnam War. Cambodia shares a several hundred-mile-long border with Vietnam, and due to its proximity, Cambodia was entwined in the Vietnam War. Do you remember the Kent State riots and the killing of university students in the US in May 1970 that was a turning point in the public perspective towards opposition to the Vietnam War? Do you remember what they were protesting on that day? Most people don't remember. They were protesting the secret bombing of Cambodia which had started under President Nixon.

Well, Noit grew up under those bombs. When kids should have been studying in school and playing in parks, this little girl was listening to the distant sounds of war growing closer and closer each day. The children would scan the sky for planes that dropped earth-shattering death from their bellies. They hoped one would not fall on them. The nightmare of American bombs often came close, nearly killing her and her family long before the Khmer Rouge could come into the city. It was impossible for Noit's mother to shield her daughter from the growing war. If it wasn't bombs falling from American bombers in the sky, it was the indiscriminate shelling and mortar attacks on Phnom Penh. The eastern border of the capital city is demarcated by the Mekong River, one of the largest rivers in the world and in some places is several miles across. Each day, Khmer Rouge soldiers would hide in the brush on the opposite bank and fire motors, rockets or small arms into the defenseless city. No one knew where the next rocket would come from, nor where it would land. Everyone felt they were a potential target. Sometimes rockets would fall on crowded markets or schools causing massive casualties. Because the war was nationwide, villagers were flooding into the city which was the last government stronghold, in an attempt to escape the Khmer Rouge advances. The schools soon closed, but the children would just cower in fear in their homes. They had no places to play or any place which was truly safe.

The toys of the children were less lethal instruments of war. Burned out tanks or army trucks became jungle gyms while colorful smoke grenades replaced toy balls. No child at that time could ever imagine a Disney movie or a cute doll. One friend, Thavy, who grew up at this time recalled how his favorite toy was colorful smoke grenades which soldiers would use to mark landing zones for incoming aircraft. His dad would bring some to the house for his kids to play with. Setting off the smoke grenade was a great thrill and they would try to guess the color before the smoke filled the sky. One day, Thavy made the mistake of setting off one inside his house. Rapidly, colorful smoke filled the entire house and began billowing out of the windows and doors. After the panic had subsided they had a good laugh as they waited outside their house for the smoke to dissipate and wondered what story they could concoct to tell his father!

It would not be long before the Khmer Rouge would take over Phnom Penh. Fear was in the air. The shelling of Phnom Penh was constant and even small fire arms could be heard throughout the day. Then one day, out of the blue, the sky was filled with helicopters. While normally children excitedly scan the skies when they hear the sound of helicopter, in this case the sight of the large transport helicopters meant fear and more hopelessness. The Americans left, just days after promising to never leave the people of Cambodia. It would only be a matter of a couple days before the Khmer Rouge entered the city. Noit was 11 years old.

April is a hot month, but it is the month of Cambodia's biggest holiday, the Khmer New Year. During this time schools shut down, businesses close and families gather together from all over Cambodia. Every community plays traditional games, has water-fights and kids play outside games constantly. The moms and dads usually sit in the shade playing cards and laughing as they chat all day long and deep into the night. The joy of the holidays would cease in 1975 as the Khmer Rouge used the time of the holiday for their final push into the city. They broke the will power of the government forces and shattered the festive spirit of the holiday. There would be no joy during the Khmer New Year holiday, nor would there be for decades to come. Children would not laugh and play and the remnant of once large families would come and recall those who were lost. A time of joy was turned into a time of pain, despair and grief.

Immediately upon entering the city on April 17, the Khmer Rouge rounded up the senior government officials, including the acting Prime Minister Long Boreth. They took them to the center of the town in what was a historic French colonial sports club called the "*Cercle Sportif*". Not only was it a place of fun and laughter with one of the only swimming pools in town, but many balls and dances were held in the colonial buildings. For generations of Phnom Penh residents this club spoke of all the joys of urban living. In 1975 it became the location that the Khmer Rouge brought the senior officials to the center of the compound and shot them, dumping their bodies in the swimming pool. There would be no more laughter and joy around that pool any longer. The officials who were slaughtered there were the ones who were left by Americans when they evacuated a few days earlier. Ironically, in 2005 the US purchased the *Cercle Sportif* from the Cambodian government and built a new US embassy on the large compound where their former Cambodian partners were executed.

Noit never had a childhood. She never had a doll. She never knew what it was like to be a restless teenager. She never had a pen pal or close friend, much less a prom to attend wearing a pretty dress. She never went on a picnic with her family nor played in a swimming pool with her cousins. She never had a boyfriend to take her to a movie and hold her hand walking along the riverside. Her childhood was lost in the violence that had overcome her country.

You Have No Family

As soon as Noit and her family left the city they were given daily work assignments until they could be assigned to a different province for work projects, in effect, concentration camps. Eventually, they were gathered together and sent to board a train bound for the north. Since they were on the east side of Phnom Penh and the train loading area was on the north side they would need to cross Phnom Penh, but as they approached the city they were forced south to bypass the city. As they circumvented the outskirts of the city they assumed that the city was functioning as normal. What they saw shocked them. The outskirts were not deserted but full of Chinese nationals. Their dress and appearance in Maoist fashion made it clear that they were Chinese nationals. It was an odd sight. As they finally arrived on the north side of Phnom Penh they were all jammed into old box cars. Each person was given one piece of bread and no water for the trip.

The box cars creaked along, baking in the hot sun, but jolting without rhythm back and forth on the uneven tracks. People were so packed together that the air was stifling and pungent with body order. Yet, everyone's skin was dry and cracking because malnutrition and dehydration had already set in. They were packed in so tightly that everyone was touching each other. No one could possibly lay down, but they sat or stood laying against each other. Along the way, soldiers would stop the slow moving train and take the new "workers" from the cars.

Though the journey would only take three to four hours by car, they were on the train an entire day and into the night. After enduring the agony of travel, the train arrived in *Pursat* Province, in the Northwest of Cambodia. Upon arriving in *Pursat*, Noit and most of her relatives were unloaded. It was already night, so they were told to sleep in an open dry rice field. There was no shelter and no one was really sure where they were or what they were sent there to do.

Early in the morning they were then loaded on ox carts to another unknown destination. Still hungry, they were herded down dirt paths. As they passed clusters of homes, they would see people in villages but no one was talking, no children playing and there was no interaction between individuals.

Upon arriving in the village the entire box car of over a hundred people was told to stay in one abandoned village house. There was no privacy, but it was all in the strategic scheme to eventually decimate the most important institution remaining in Cambodia; the family. After a few days of being jammed into a small space, the Khmer Rouge provided a "solution" to their discomfort by providing food and accommodations by age group rather than by families. Mothers went with one group. Young mothers and little infants in another group. Young men and women were separated into different groups, and teenagers in another. Noit, being 11 years old and a tiny little girl, was placed in a children's group. With tears in her eyes, she was taken away from those she loved. As Noit was pulled away from her family, she felt as if her heart would explode. Now, she was truly alone.

Noit was held near the banks of Cambodia's great lake. The lake is called *"Tonle Sap"* in Cambodia which unimaginatively means "fresh water river". Its dry season surface area is 2,500 km^2 (965 mi^2). But, this is a very unusual lake which is affected by the geology of Cambodia. Cambodia is extremely flat, with small hills surrounding its borders. All the water in Cambodia flows to its center. The only "exit point" for water is down the Mekong River which completes its 2,500 mile flow from Tibet by bypassing Cambodia. Throughout most of Cambodia the massive force of the river digs up silt and soil and churns them with the murky water as the river travels throughout the journey across the country. While the river usually appears brown with this silt, it is along its banks that the most fertile soil in Cambodia is found.   Because of the lack of major topography, when the Mekong River grows in flow and depth during the rainy season, it actually becomes higher than the lake, causing it to flood. The *Tonle Sap* then fills and grows at least seven times its size, encompassing most of central Cambodia. Its flooded surface area can be 16,000 km^2 (6,178 mi^2), putting its size in the top twenty lakes in the world, and the largest in Southeast Asia. During half the year the barren dry fields can be 2-3 meters (6-10 feet) deep in water! For centuries the kings and rulers of Cambodia have tried, mostly in vain, to harness the fresh water potential for irrigation and economic development. This is one of the reasons why nearly all traditional homes are built on stilts. However, as Noit peered across the paddies and looked for signs of life in various homes she saw an eerie sight. Every home appeared to be empty. The walls, windows and doors had all been ripped off. It was as if the entire population of Cambodia had vanished.

Though Noit was in a group of many kids, she never felt so alone. Fear gripped her along with overwhelming confusion. In the village with the other children Noit learned how to survive. She saw others leaning down into the muddy creek and pressing their *karma* scarves into the water slowly, and then sucking up the water. The scarf acted somewhat like a filter, but only blocking larger chucks of dirt and insects. Noit's thirst was so great and her hunger pangs so strong, it didn't matter. She also knelt and followed the others sucking up some water into her mouth. Soon, as a dirt taste filled her mouth the hunger pangs went away. Soon thereafter, black clad soldiers holding clubs and guns screamed at them to get away from the creek and follow them. The small children huddled together like a panicked herd of sheep. No leader, no direction, just wandering in a group as it provided some security. The children were shown a long palm leaf covered shelter. There were no walls and it was barely tall enough for these young children to stand in. It has a dirt floor with nothing inside. This would be Noit's home for the next four years.

In the evening they were gathered into groups for their re-education classes. Here they were told that everything they had learned, everything they had held in their culture had been polluted by the West, imperialism, and the Vietnamese. Additionally, they were told that they no longer had a family, but *Ongka* would be their new family. (*Ongka* is the common term for which the Khmer Rouge referred to itself. The word simply means an "organization".)

Each night Noit would return to a large makeshift hut where all the other children would be kept. Though they would sleep late at night they would be awakened before dawn each day and walk to their working location. The morning marches were long and in complete silence. They were always up before the sun and stumbled along uneven and narrow rice paddy walls. She learned to never draw attention to herself or speak up. Silence and anonymity were survival lessons. No one knew what their task was from day to day, not what the Khmer Rouge expected them to do. Everything seemed spontaneous without any direction. Indeed, history would show that while the Khmer Rouge architects had great plans for water irrigation, increasing rice harvests and developing agriculture technology, there were few specific details. After walking for an hour or more they would arrive at the daily work site. A site, which was typically so isolated they rarely ever saw any other people, and they would do as the young soldiers demanded; Grow rice, dig water canals, repair rice paddies, or pick out weeds from growing rice. Throughout every moment fear gripped them. They could be killed at any time, for any reason. Life seemed completely random and utterly meaningless. Soon, everyone had lost track of the days, weeks and months. Every day was the same regardless of the weather. Work was all they knew.

As a small girl, Noit was sent off each day before the break of dawn to work, sometimes walking for hours, across rice paddies and bushes to new work sites. They would often see other work crews such as teenagers or adults, but they were not allowed to speak to them or interact with them. They were only to do their assigned task for the day. In the rainy season, they would be assigned to planting rice and pulling weeds. Other times, they dug water canals and hauled dirt to make village roads. They would only be given a few short rest breaks and no food during the day. The noonday heat was nearly unbearable, but they were still required to work. Sometimes Noit would see paddy crabs, little fish, and even insects and want to eat them so her body could get even a minute amount of nutrients. But, she knew that if anyone saw her eat them she would be branded as a traitor of the State. During the evening brainwashing sessions, the people would be encouraged to report anything they saw others do. This behavior turned the whole country into spies and people would be betrayed by their own friends and family. Soon, the idea of friends and even family disintegrated and fear and suspicion ruled the country. No one could be trusted.

Those found guilty of stealing, which often amounted to merely catching earthworms or picking leaves from the trees to eat, would be tortured in front of the group. Sometimes they would be left for dead, but more commonly, they would be dragged out of the village at night, never to be seen again. Their bodies would be discarded with those who had been punished before them. One time, Noit's eyes witnessed a horrible spectacle. One lady in the village, out of desperation, secretly beat a child to death and brought the bloodied body back to the village in a rice sack. Secretly, she cooked the child and shared the meat with others. Desperation had set in. When the Khmer Rouge found out about the cannibalism they bound the lady and anyone who was suspected of eating the child as well.

The Khmer Rouge believed in collective punishment of the society and would often say, "If you want to kill a weed, you have to remove the roots." And by this, the people knew that they would kill entire families for the "crime" of one member. In this cannibalism case, they decided to exact such a punishment. The young Khmer Rouge soldiers went village by village to find every relative of the lady who cannibalized the child, and in front of everyone, they were summarily executed... their family lineage expunged for all time.

Every day was dominated by the fear of death. Every day was filled with backbreaking work. Every day was filled with starvation and hunger. Every moment Noit just tried to survive a little longer.

Chapter 6

"A day will come when we will chase a dog because he has a grain of rice stuck on his tail." -- Neang Bunnak, Noit's Grandmother

This quote may have a strange sound to it, but this was a prophecy which Noit's grandmother had in her heart many years before war broke out in Cambodia. She recalled it many times to her children and even grandchildren. Noit loved her grandmother dearly. She would sit and talk to her for hours sharing whatever thoughts came into her mind. When her grandmother would make food for the family, Noit would always want to help her with the preparations. However, during the meal her grandmother would insist they eat every last grain of rice off their plate. They were often perplexed by her insistence because there was always enough. Each day at meal time Noit's grandmother would repeatedly say, "Be careful when you eat. If you spill your rice, you must pick it up and eat it all". Whenever they didn't respond to her encouragement to clean their plates she would repeat again, "A day will come when we will chase a dog because he has a grain of rice stuck on his tail." She constantly warned them that they needed to be ready for one day when there would be starvation.

Noit's grandmother had survived through the early 1940's during WWII when Japan seized "de-facto" control of Cambodia. She had also lived through a near civil war called the *Issarak Rebellion* in the 1940's and 1950's which was an anti-colonial uprising which became a precursor to the Khmer Rouge. Noit's grandfather, Houn, was killed during this violent uprising. The loss was so painful to his wife she buried it deep in her heart and never spoke about the details surrounding his killing. It was likely the memory that was burned in her of a horrible and difficult time that she feared would return. Those days of the *Isaarak Rebellion* had been difficult times, but the rule of the Khmer Rouge would be far worse for her grandmother to bear and somehow she had some foreshadowing of it.

Finally, that day she dreaded did come. In early 1975, the Maoist Khmer Rouge finally took over Phnom Penh after a decade of guerilla fighting, sealing their control over the entire land of Cambodia. Their retribution would be swift and severe. All city people were to be used as instruments of the redevelopment of Cambodia. Their lives were of no value to the Khmer Rouge except for the building of water canals and planting rice. Because they had no value, the *Ongka* would waste no bullets on their execution, nor any food on their survival.

In early 1976, when Noit's grandmother saw the situation, she knew that the prophecy she had ringing in her heart for so many years would come true. Once they separated all the family members from each other they instituted a "communal" feeding scheme where each person would only get one limited meal per day. Having lived through previous hardship during times of war and rebellion she knew the hardship which was coming. For her, this policy was the last straw. All hope and the will to live vanished into hopelessness. She decided not to eat and just die as quickly as possible. Starvation is a horrible way to die. Soon, her legs were so swollen she could no longer walk. At night, the pain caused her to scream. The screams echoed across the village and pierced the ears of her granddaughter Noit. Though Noit was held in a separate area from her other family members, she soon discovered that some of her family members were held in nearby villages according to their age and work assignments. However, Noit was close enough to hear the cries of her grandmother. Sometimes she would sneak into the night to sit by her side, though to be caught would have been instant death. Noit's little heart was torn to shreds hearing the pain of her beloved grandmother writhing in pain. She would sometimes sneak in to her grandmother's shelter and rub her grandmother's legs and comfort her in any way she could, including saving a few grains of rice from her portion; however, her grandmother refused to eat. One night the screaming was intense and she could hear the piercing sounds call out, "I am hungry, I need rice." Then late that night, the screams went silent. Dread came over Noit as she feared the worst. Noit's little body was so beaten down by starvation and overwork that her eyes could not even make tears. Her heart was burning inside her chest with the thought of this immense loss.

In the morning, Noit and her brother snuck away from their village and went to where their grandmother was. Indeed, her beloved grandmother was gone. Noit was overcome with grief seeing her lifeless body. A Khmer Rouge soldier saw her grieving and shouted, "What good will it do for you to cry? Do you want to join her?" The pain of such harsh indifference burned into Noit's soul. Together with her brother they tried to dig a hole to bury their grandmother. They were unable to dig the hole very deep because they were so weak, but they managed to cover her body with a little dirt. One by one over the next four years, her brother, other siblings, aunts and uncles and cousins would die of starvation and exhaustion, and their bodies would be unceremoniously scattered among the bushes where wild dogs and vultures would rip them apart.

Noit felt even more alone. She pondered that she would never get to hug her mother, father or siblings again, much less taste the wonderful food or laugh and giggle as she played with her grandmother. To this day, she will never leave a grain of rice on her plate.

Hell

Three years, eight months and twenty days. Every day under the Khmer Rouge was like living in hell.

All of the food, what little there was, was taken to a central cooking area. A few older women were selected as the cooks for Village Six, originally called *O Bot* which means a "creek bend". Sure enough the village sits on the bend of a dry creek bed which only has water in the flooding season. Everyone worked, even the mothers with infants and those under five years old. The oldest grandmothers in the village were assigned to take care of the babies while everyone else worked.

It was difficult work for educated city residents who had no experience in hard physical labor. Cambodia is a very hot country with average daily temperature around 95 degrees (32°C). During the dry season it can easily reach over 100 degrees (38°C) each day. The elements are a harsh environment for someone who has not be conditioned to work in such an environment. In *Ongka's* new society everyone was obliged to work. Every project was deemed to put the nation closer to an agrarian utopia. Perhaps some of the projects might have succeeded had it not been for the fact that at the end of a strenuous day they hungrily returned to their commune only to be fed a thin rice broth, their only meal for the day.

At the beginning of each year the village was given its full-year's rice supply. However, the volume was never more than what would feed the people for a single month. One cup of rice had to feed twenty-two people per day. The rice was finely ground and cooked in a large quantity of water. They would often put leaves and even cut the stocks of banana trees to put into it to try and add any nutrients to the communal food. In fact, what they were eating was not food fit for humans, but mere pig feed.

Occasionally when there was no rice, one cup of ground corn would be boiled and given for the group to share. The only ones in the village who were allowed to eat on their own in the village or in homes were rural uneducated farmers who were deemed useful to the Khmer Rouge cause and supportive of the Khmer Rouge. Those who had to eat from group community pots were simply slave labor and prisoners who had no value except for use as physical labor. They were only to be kept alive with the absolutely bare minimum of resources. There was no intent that they would survive.

Sickness was rampant. Medicine was non-existent. The death count mounted as starvation and disease took their ultimate toll. The situation in Noit's village was not unique. Clearly they were operating with an extermination strategy as every community in Cambodia was run the same way. One day Noit became very sick and was told to go to a makeshift hospital. Noit yearned for her mother, or anyone to love and care for her when she was sick, but no one came. All she received was callous treatment from the heartless Khmer Rouge. She had observed that people who went to the hospital died, so she refused. She forced herself back to the rice fields. There was no alternative. The choice was to go to the hospital to die, or to work, perhaps dying there in the fields. Later, she was working in a field on a hot day, clearing weeds and removing soil. The Khmer Rouge soldier had assigned her and some other children to move twelve cubic meters of soil in one day. Failure would lead to severe punishment. In fear they worked until their young bodies felt as if they could move no more. Then Noit, swinging the large adult size hoe to get another scoop of dirt, accidentally hit her own foot instantly causing a gaping wound. The only thing she could do was to tie her *karma* scarf around her foot. Soon it was drenched with blood. As the shock of the accident wore off the pain set in. But there was no reprieve, no rest and no provision for accidents. She had to continue the backbreaking work, only now she was under the close wicked watch of the Khmer Rouge soldiers who were just waiting for a stumble, a fall, or anything to slow her pace in any way which would give an opening for them to finish her off. It was as if their evil minds were seeking to kill as sport.

She managed to survive the day. At night hobbling home she ate her bit of rice and then soaked the bloody *karma* into some muddy creek water and tried to clean the wound. She cut off a chuck of her hair and put it into the wound trying to stop the bleeding. It would barely scab over and insects and flies would gather at the festering wound. Because of the lack of nutrition in her body it remained an open wound for nearly two years. She was in constant pain from the wound, when finally a lady offered her some traditional medical advice. She told Noit to catch a poisonous toad and beat it until the white poison comes out. Put the poison into the wound and it will heal. Noit was willing to try anything. She soon found a toad and killed it, beating its back as the white poison oozed out. She then pressed the poison into the wound. It burned horribly as the poison touched the wound. She wanted to scream with pain. It burned for more than a day until it just quit. To her amazement, some tender red flesh began to form over the wound. Within a week the pain of the long-time injury was gone. The toad's poison apparently worked.

The village that began with twenty-seven families was becoming very quiet. All around Noit, people were dying. The young, black pajama-like clad soldiers would carry the bodies away each day. The people did not know where they were being taken to. The mass graves, containing hundreds of human skeletons, would be discovered all across the country many years later. Most likely there are still hundreds of mass graves which have never been discovered.

Most people died of starvation. It was a horrible death. The memory of the screams coming from the little huts, all over the village, still haunts Noit's memory. The first signs that death was close was swelling of the extremities, especially the legs. They would lose use of their legs and later often become paralyzed. Just before a person died they would scream with all their remaining energy, just like Noit's grandmother did. Soon the screaming would stop, they were gone. Noit remembers one day hearing a man screaming in a nearby house. The screaming seemed to be getting closer to them, but he could not walk. They couldn't help anyway, they had no food themselves. Then they saw the man, dragging himself along the ground in front of their little hut. He was screaming as loud as he

could for help. Right in front of her, he stopped moving, laying in the dirt and did not utter a sound. He was dead. Death and its pungent smell filled the air.

Noit's brother died even more traumatically. Being older than Noit he was sent to the dreaded *Kong Chalat* (young people's unit). They were the strongest in the society so they were worked the hardest. After only a few weeks away Noit saw her brother walking down the road. He looked like death had already swallowed him. His face, eyes and body were emaciated. He had run away fearing death and had gone to find his mother. Noit's mother tried to force some grains of rice into his mouth, but his throat could not swallow them. Quietly, he whispered to his mom, "I'm sorry, Mommy. Please forgive me for being a bad son. I'm sorry." He would repeat it over and over again until he grew quiet. Noit's mother, broken-hearted, dared not to even look into his face and watch her son die. There was nothing she could do for him except hide him from the roaming Khmer Rouge soldiers. Noit secretly found her way to his side before he died. The echo of his dying words, "I'm sorry, mommy" as if he was guilty of anything sunk her heart to its lowest depths.

After he took his last breath, she stayed beside him for three days and nights. No one would help carry his body away. The Khmer Rouge would force other villages to remove dead bodies from the villages under threat of not allowing them to eat, but even so they tried to avoid removing bodies. There was so much death that no one wanted to remove any more bodies. Burying dead bodies was also someone's punishment and if there wasn't a direct order to bury a specific body, it was a task that was easily skipped. Noit was too small and weak to move her big brother's body. Noit's mother, also struggling with the effects of starvation, could hardly walk because of badly swollen legs. She strained to remove the body of her precious lifeless son, but there were no more surviving family members capable of helping.

Noit's mother placed the best shirt and pants she could find on the body of her son for his burial. As some men walked by the house she begged them to help bury her son. The men finally agreed, but seeing the clothes on the body, they quickly removed them and left, without burying the body. Again Noit's mother dressed her naked son with more tattered clothes. The men returned, beginning once again to steal the clothes. Noit's mother pleaded with the men to bury her son, only then, if she agreed she would give them all the clothes she had when the task was completed. The men finally agreed. There was no compassion and no dignity in those days.

They loaded the body on a cow-drawn cart, and seemed to have been gone perhaps only two or three minutes when they returned to get all of the additional clothing. They knew that their loved one had not been properly buried. The men had not gone far, probably throwing the body into one of the mass graves where all the bodies of the victims of the cruel Khmer Rouge were dumped.

As starvation claimed more and more victims, people became more and more desperate for food. The Khmer Rouge themselves were not starving though. Some of them were even fat! The Khmer Rouge cook was a fat lady who helped herself to as much food as she wanted, even though she carefully divided up the rice... one cup for twenty-two for the "city people".

By the end of the first year, the number remaining alive in Village Six were only eight. Noit, as a young child, was one of the eight who had miraculously survived insurmountable horror: the hunger, sickness, forced labor, and losses beyond comprehension.

The people stoically internalized their grief. No criticism of the new regime was tolerated. Tears were not allowed. Showing emotion meant sure death. To cry out in pain or anguish would result in being removed and never be seen again. If a loved one died, no tears were to be shed or that person would join their loved one very quickly.

Uniformity of appearance was also forced. The long beautiful dark hair of the women and young girls was cropped. Everyone dressed only in long sleeved black shirts to hide their tan-skinned arms. The girls were taught that it was a shame not to keep them covered. Everyone wore black, modeled after the Maoist clothing of the Cultural Revolution in China. Men, women, youth or children, all were dressed in black clothes which soon turned to rags under the blazing sun.

One of Noit's work assignments, along with the nine other girls in her group, ranging from ages seven to fifteen, was to clean the rice fields of weeds after being plowed by the men. It was hard work, walking in the mud and water, bending down to her feet pulling out the unwanted weeds and other organic material that had to be removed before planting could begin.

The fact that rice was Cambodia's largest source of foreign exchange formed the basis for the economic policies of the Khmer Rouge, which emphasized the development of agriculture. The Khmer Rouge planned to dramatically increase the country's rice production. In theory the foreign currency earned would finance imports of farm machinery and fertilizer, and thereby help make the country self-sufficient. The government's goal and slogan was "three tons [of harvested rice] per hectare." This meant tripling the average yield throughout the country, with only four years allowed to achieve this miracle. The plan, however, ignored the facts: Cambodia was just emerging from five devastating years of war and there was a shortage of tools, seed and livestock. Though they harvested rice for *Ongka* they were not allowed to eat it. Most was shipped to China in exchange for weapons leaving only a meager supply for Cambodia. It was a plan designed by demons to destroy the nation. It was a goal which could never have been achieved.

Noit's labor group was generally awakened between three or four in the morning. The unmerciful hour depended on the distance they would have to walk that day to reach the rice field needing to be cleaned. Sometimes they walked three or four hours simply to reach the fields where they were to work. They were never allowed to travel on roads and so were forced to trudge through swamps, canals, and overgrown brush and rice paddies. Upon arrival, they worked until the hot mid-day sun and were given a short break. After the break, they would not stop until just before the sun went down. The Khmer Rouge soldiers watched the children all the time to make sure they were working. There was no unscheduled rest, and no such thing as play. It seemed they were always forced to work in fields far from the place they were to sleep. When they arrived late at night to sleep, they frequently had to listen to indoctrination sessions. Weakened in body and spirit, most of the people meekly received the instructions.

At the end of their work-day, there were times when the little children were too exhausted to walk back to the village. They simply laid on the thin muddy embankments around the paddies. At these times they would sometimes be awakened in the middle of the night to go back to work in the fields by the moonlight, or to walk three or four hours more to the next rice fields. They were expected to work yet they were being fed almost nothing.

During the two-hour rest time each day, Noit carefully moved away from the others, trying to catch small paddy crabs, fish or frogs in nearby water. She regularly plucked leaves, eating them for their life-giving nutrients. A few other children would do the same, but with great care. If caught searching for food, the guards would hit the children and yell terribly frightening, threatening things at them. Everything was the property of *Ongka* and even picking a leaf off a tree was stealing from *Ongka*. Punishment was harsh, at times leading to death. No one would ever think of stealing any fruits or vegetables, those were reserved for the Khmer Rouge soldiers and the officials of *Ongka*.

During the evening meetings the children were required to confess if anyone had committed a wrong that day, such as going near the water to find something to eat. Noit on many occasions had to confess she had done just that, going against the Khmer Rouge laws governing their new society. Noit would seek forgiveness for her wrongful behavior, and repeat the required statement, "Please correct me". She would be severely reprimanded for her behavior, cursed at and ordered never to do it again. But another day would come when the hunger pains were so great she would slip away again and again to find food to keep alive. Day in and day out as one year became two, two became three, and three became four, Noit endured the harsh, laborious conditions of Pol Pot's Khmer Rouge rule. She lived in constant fear. It was hell.

Every day was the same. No one knew what day it was, and if they claimed to know, they were lying. There were no holidays, no rest days, no festivals, nor any celebrations of completed projects. They only knew what the general seasons were. February to May are dry, but intensely hot months. June through October are extremely wet with daily monsoonal rain showers. During those times the entire village was surrounded by water from the expanding great lake. November through January are dry, but cooler months. As months passed, and seasons circulated they realized they would never escape this hell except by death. They worked and worked every day and had a meaningless existence.

Their numbers continued to dwindle. Of the twenty seven families, consisting of several hundred people who were sent into this isolated village in *Bakan* district, few survived. Noit's mind became numb and dull. Without any stimulant other than work and the terror the Khmer Rouge instilled in their hearts, there was nothing to think about. There was no news, no information of relevance. Today Cambodian's often refer to themselves as being like frogs deep in a well. This is the source of that analogy. The communists purposely isolated itself from the world, allowing only a few like-minded oppressive communist governments to send representatives into the country, such as North Korea, Cuba, Bulgaria, Yugoslavia and the USSR. Nationally, they also limited contact with other villages or regions to limit any information spreading on the state of the country. They didn't want villages to have any means to contact anyone else so that they could not form any alliances or potentially rise up against their captors.

Noit only did as she was expected and hoped to never draw attention to herself. Sometimes, though, she would try to run away. She tried it one time early on in her captivity in hopes of finding her mother who was moved to a different village. When she was out searching she came across some elderly grandmothers who were left to die. They were considered worthless to the cause, so abandoned to die. They were clearly starving to death. They enjoyed talking to Noit and seeing this little girl named Noit. They probably projected the memories of their grandchildren onto little Noit. As she sat with them she saw movement in the grass nearby. Quickly she pounced into the tall weeds and came back a few seconds later with a small crab. She immediately gave the small coin-sized crab to the grandmothers to eat. They were so grateful because they were much too old and malnourished to be able to find any food, much less catch a scampering crab. Noit knew she could not stay long, but occasionally she would slip away from her group during the heat of the day and try to catch some worms, pick leaves or catch more crabs for the grandmothers. Though it could have cost her life, it gave her life some meaning to be able to serve others who could not help themselves. Indeed, she was starving, but maybe helping others provided energy for her own life.

During each year, there was one time that Noit had to learn a painful lesson. The Khmer Rouge were trying to increase rice yields by enslaving the whole nation. Although they built huge irrigation projects, the fields still only had enough water for one crop per year. The crop was usually harvested after the end of the rainy season. As they brought in the first rice harvest of the year, the Khmer Rouge would announce that everyone could eat as much rice as they wanted as a way to celebrate. The older young people and adults would fight to get to the food first. The smell of freshly cooked rice lofted through the air as a nearly uncontrollable urge to devour the rice would overcome them. The oldest and strongest would get the rice first and force down handful after handful of rice.

Somehow they thought that by stuffing themselves with rice they could make up for the year's worth of rice they hadn't gotten. However, within a few minutes they were moaning in pain, writhing on the ground. It was as if they were being poisoned and they were dying from the inside out. Within a short amount of time, they usually died. The Khmer Rouge soldiers could be seen joking and laughing about the way they died. It seemed to be a sickening trick to kill more people. Their bodies had been so starved, they could not eat full meals. Doing so would kill them and the Khmer Rouge certainly knew this. When Noit saw this, she was again tormented. She was so hungry and the smell of the rice was intoxicating, but she had to resist eating more than a fist size of rice. She would eat a bit and immediately leave the area to savor the taste in her mouth, but avoid eating too much.

Being in the remote western province Noit was far from any road, so she never saw vehicles of any kind for years. She never saw the train again either since it had dropped her off late at night many years previously. She never saw any aircraft or smoke trails in the sky that airplanes made. Every day, their jobs would change, but it was always the same. They would walk a far distance, work all day and then walk all the way back. They rarely saw anyone else when they were walking. They never walked through a village or on main roads so they did not know what could be happening outside of the remote *Bakan* district.

However, late into the third year of captivity they could sense something was amiss. The Khmer Rouge soldiers would often meet together and sometimes they would see groups of other soldiers moving quickly through their area. Their work never changed, but it just seemed as though something was not right. Then, during the harvest time (which they would learn was late 1978 and early 1979) an uneasiness was clearly observed amongst the Khmer Rouge captors. The captives would be asked to get up, gather all their belongings (which wasn't more than a karma and an extra shirt) and told they were to leave the village. They would start their move and then the Khmer Rouge would tell them to stop and wait as if something was supposed to happen. This took place a few times in early 1979 as the hot season came over them.

The group of children which was once more than a hundred children were now just down to a handful. The few adults that had survived looked like walking skeletons. Their eyes were sunken deep into their skulls and it was as if they had no muscles in their bodies, only bones. Their skin was black and leathery. While the city people had once kept themselves covered from the oppressiveness of the sun in order to keep their skin fair and tender, they now appeared like the sandpapery black skin of water buffalo. They didn't sweat, even though it was so oppressively hot. They didn't have enough moisture in their body to activate sweat glands.

Then, breaking up their meaningless days, a final announcement came to them again: "Pack up, this time everyone has to leave. Our jobs here are done."

They were confused as some fields still had unharvested rice, but they had long given up questioning or even trying to understand the orders given by the uneducated peasant army. They quickly gathered their things and began to walk. As they walked toward other villages they could see other villagers gathering their things and leaving too. They were all heading one direction: toward the western mountains. Why? They did not know, but they just walked.

Automatically, when we hear the words, "A savior is born," today we might think about Christmas and Jesus Christ being born into the world. His miraculous birth led the way for our eternal salvation from sin. However, this story is about a little nameless baby that was born in a roadside hut in the *Bakan* district, *Pursat* province in Cambodia, during the genocidal reign of the Khmer Rouge.

After nearly four years under Khmer Rouge control, the entire nation was one giant concentration camp and everyone, including the Khmer Rouge themselves were enslaved. The elite Khmer Rouge leadership had begun nation-wide purges of their own loyal comrades as fear and suspicion, which they created in order to control the populaces, seeped into their own minds. Bodies littered every field in *Bakan* district. There were no graves, just convenient ditches and bushes to dump bodies into. Wild animals ripped apart the flesh of decomposing bodies, and limbs were scattered everywhere. There was no shielding their eyes from the horrible sight of genocide, the stench of death and the sight of dismembered bodies were in plain view.

Unknown to Noit, on December 2nd of 1978, at the peak of the harvest season when the wet monsoons ceased, the Vietnamese army, along with some Cambodian forces under General Heng Samrin had launched an invasion into Cambodia. It took only a few weeks for tanks to roll into the deserted city of Phnom Penh on January 7, 1979 to reclaim the city. The Khmer Rouge had never used the city in any significant capacity. They continued meeting in jungle hideouts and only had a few officers stationed in the city giving the appearance of a functioning central government.

By April of 1979, only the top Khmer Rouge leaders knew that their absolute control was coming to an end. Villagers had no idea that the Vietnamese and Khmer Liberation Army were fighting to remove the Khmer Rouge - province by province and village by village. The armies had come from the southeast of the country and were fighting their way village by village toward the northwest. The final desperate response of the Khmer Rouge was to execute as many witnesses of their reign as they could through mass execution.

In Noit's village prison of *O Bot*, the Khmer Rouge leaders received orders to move everyone to the western mountains. A great march was on. After four years of starvation, torture and death, they somehow knew that they were being marched to their final execution. Few cared. Death would be a release from pain. Amazingly, Noit's little brother, Sit, now nearly ten years old, was brought to Noit's village and they were re-united. Each year, she had seen her mother only briefly and knew that her older sister was also somewhere in the area too. All her other relatives and family had already died. Noit marched along with her children's group. They were not walking in an orderly manner, just in small clumps of victims. The Khmer Rouge leaders often moved much faster and would give the group instructions to meet down the road after a few hours walking. Sometimes the Khmer Rouge leaders rode by horseback, moving much faster than the others. During the march westward Noit found her mother in another group. When Noit saw her mother, the reunion was bittersweet. Emotion was forbidden as was any recognition of kinship. Remarkably, just a few hours later, she found her sister hiding. She had left the teenage group and knew if she was caught the punishment would be death. The Khmer Rouge had specifically divided up the families so they would have no one to help them. Now, for the first time in nearly four years the surviving members of a once large family were reunited. There was no joy or laughter as they knew they were being marched to their final reunion in death. At least they would be together. A mother, two daughters and a young son. While they should look healthy and strong, they were skinny and weak. But, they were alive.

Along the road, they found themselves falling behind the group. This made the Khmer Rouge leaders angry, but they kept pressing the people ahead, often moving up ahead of the group. At one point, Noit and her mother were thinking of trying to stop for the night rather than continue walking hours more. There was a little abandoned hut along the roadside which they decided to duck into and wait for dark. A few minutes after they entered the little hut another girl and young man also came inside. The girl was visibly pregnant and, with her moaning and groaning, was likely in labor.

Noit's mother helped the girl get as comfortable as she could on a makeshift bamboo bed. They huddled quietly in the hut hoping that all the people walking would pass them by without realizing their absence. Within a few hours a new baby girl was born. Almost immediately after the birth a Khmer Rouge cadre stuck his head into the little hut. They all feared death as they had broken away from the main group. When he looked into the hut he immediately blurted out a curse word at them. Then he saw the newborn baby. Angrily, he told them to move on in a few hours after the young woman got some rest from the delivery. He moved away and they were alone in the hut. Each one drifted to sleep, along with Noit next to her mother who had helped deliver a new baby into a horrible world.

Long before dawn, they awoke to the sound of people moving back down the road away from the mountains in the opposite direction. Those returning said that the Khmer Rouge seemed to be more chaotic than usual and they were not sure whether to go on to the mountains or to go back to the village, so some had decided to head back toward the village rather than finishing the trek to the mountains.

The delay due to the birth had saved them critical time. Many of those who had completed the march were being executed in the distant jungle hills. Nearly the entire village of *O Bot* had already been put to death. But the Khmer Rouge had realized that some were not coming to the mountains and so soldiers were sent back to execute all stragglers.

Because of the birth of the child in that little hut, they were saved from death once again. After resting for a couple of days Noit and her little brother decided to play. They had almost forgotten how to play, but from natural instincts they began to run around the fields playing with any interesting object they could find. They found a piece of metal roofing and laid on it looking into the hot sky with clouds forming overhead. For a moment they transcended the hell from which they lived. As they laid on the metal, a sprinkle hit them in the face. Then another and another. In the middle of April it is very unusual to have any rain at all. Soon there was a downpour. Noit and her brother Sit kept laying in the rain thinking it would only last a moment, but it rained for what seemed to be an hour. Soon, Noit and her brother were shivering in the cold. Noit's mother feared they would catch a cold and die.

As soon as the rain finished, Noit's mother told everyone they should move back toward the village. The best way to dry the kids out and keep them warm would be to walk again. So, the family moved on, trying to head back to *O Bot* village.

However, upon approaching the crossing of the main road they heard a commotion. They were never allowed near the main national road because the Khmer Rouge wanted to keep all their movements secret. They heard vehicles approaching; a sound which they had not heard for nearly four years. They hid in the bushes alongside the road, fearing they would be discovered and executed. As the vehicles pulled up, fear pierced their souls. They knew if they were discovered they would be killed for being separated from the group.

The vehicles stopped. They had been discovered! Then they heard a strange voice in broken Cambodian. "Do you know where Pol Pot is?" No one had ever heard of Pol Pot. They only knew the Khmer Rouge as *Ongka*. These were not Khmer Rouge soldiers. They were not even Cambodian. They were Vietnamese soldiers. They were looking for "Pol Pot". Since Noit had never heard the name Pol Pot and they were Vietnamese trying to speak a few words of Cambodian, she thought they were looking for "Skaw Pout". "Skaw Pout" is sugar palm juice. Noit pointed to the next village which had sugar palm trees and the soldiers hurried off. As they left, the soldiers told them,

"You are free now. You can go home." And just like that, in a moment, their captivity was over.

The birth of a little baby girl in the midst of genocide allowed for Noit and her family to be saved. They later learned that the Khmer Rouge soldiers did come back to look for them, but when it started raining, the soldiers didn't have any cover. They waited out the rain storm and then headed back to the mountains. This allowed just enough time for Noit and her family to make it back to the main highway where they were freed by the advancing Vietnamese army. It was sometime in April of 1979, a full four years since they were forced from their home in Phnom Penh.

Was it really over? Could they really go home? How would they get home? All of a sudden their minds became active again and they began to think.

Noit, her mother, sister and brother stood on the road in a state of shock and watched the Vietnamese army trucks move on. The day they left the city, there was a small army of family members... grandmother, aunt's uncles, brother and sisters, cousins, nephews, nieces, but now they were four and with their present physical condition, may not last much longer. They had no possessions of value, but they had each other. There was nothing to retrieve from the hut, no possessions to gather, no friends to say good-bye to... so, they just began to walk. They headed south, toward their distant home in Phnom Penh. They didn't have the energy to go very fast or very far, so they just went a short way and then slept next to the road. Eventually they came to a larger village, *Svay Dongkeo*, where more people were emerging from the little villages nearby as their Khmer Rouge captors slipped away into the mountains. In *Svay Dongkeo* they gathered with hundreds of other survivors and talked about what to do next. Vietnamese troops continued to move through the area. Occasionally, they would hear distant shots ring out, but basically the Khmer Rouge were fleeing as fast as they could and the main fighting was reported to be toward the Thailand border which had heavy jungle and mountains to provide cover.

Then they saw the strangest thing: two men riding on horses! They looked healthy and strong and their clothes were not torn. Who were they? The others had seen them too. The adults did not wonder who they were, they knew. They were their oppressors, Khmer Rouge soldiers trying to mix among the population and pretend they were just regular citizens. A mob formed quickly and they began beating the two just a few feet in front of Noit. Noit just stood and looked on emotionless. A small group of Vietnamese soldiers jumped in and tried to stop the beatings. One of the men could no longer stand and the people kept beating and kicking him, so the Vietnamese gave up on trying to rescue him. They were able to get the people away from the other one though. The soldiers had machine guns so no one was getting too close, but they threated the soldiers, "If you protect him, then we will kill you too!"

The Vietnamese soldier oddly tried to reason with them saying, "Let's give him a chance. Let him run and then after counting to ten I'll shoot at him."

The man, knowing his window of escape was short immediately broke through the crowed and started running.

"Một, hai, ba, . . .", the soldier slowly counted.

The Khmer Rouge man was getting away quickly and the people were quickly losing patience. The people screamed for the soldier to shoot, but it was if he was purposefully letting the Khmer Rouge soldier escape. One man lurched at the Vietnamese soldier and snatched his AK-47 out of his hands. He pointed the gun toward the man who was getting further and further away each second.

Bam, bam. . . Bam, bam, bam. . . The man dropped.

The crowd cheered and ran toward their former captor. The Vietnamese pulled back afraid of being killed by the mob. Both men were now dead, but the pent up pain of four years was not so easily satisfied. One by one the people cursed the dead bodies and hit them with whatever object they could find. Soon, the corpses were unrecognizable blobs of blood and tissue. Having nothing left to get their revenge on, the people moved away from the bodies. Noit, now a 15 year old girl, saw everything and the level of violence shocked her, even after all she had been through in the last four years. The bodies were left as they had left many of their victims, just lying discarded on the side of the road.

Soon thereafter, Noit's mother decided that there would probably be no assistance and to stay in the large group may not be safe. They left *Svay Dongkeo* and would search abandoned houses for food and materials as they walked. They continued their journey finding two cows and four chickens that had been left abandoned as the Khmer Rouge rapidly fled the advancing Vietnamese. These would become very important for their continual survival. Though they were "liberated", they quickly discovered that they had much to fear from the advancing Vietnamese army too. The first encounter with trouble came from Vietnamese soldiers demanding food. Upon seeing Vietnamese troops the Cambodians assumed they came to massacre the remaining Cambodians and take over their country. The Vietnamese and the Cambodians have been historical enemies for hundreds of years. At the sight of each group of soldiers, intense fear overcame Noit. She did not want to anger them and end up being raped, tortured or killed. As they learned from surviving the Khmer Rouge, they needed to give whatever was demanded of them with no complaints. Their goal was to remain anonymous and not stand out. Noit's mother gave them the biggest chicken and some coconuts which they had secured to their cow and they were allowed to safely proceed. They moved along as quickly as they could, always keeping their eyes pointed toward the ground.

Soon they came upon more Vietnamese soldiers wanting food as well. Another chicken was given. As darkness fell each night, Noit, her mother, brother, sister, two cows and any remaining chickens slept on the main road until the light began to bring in a new day, so they could continue their journey. They were still plagued by incessant fears as they continued to walk down the road day by day.

The numbers of people on the road increased as did the Vietnamese soldiers. They also discovered that many people were heading to Thailand to try and get away from the Vietnamese as well. Rumors were rampant that the Vietnamese were beheading all the Cambodians that they came across and were taking all the land for Vietnam. They did not know the way to Thailand, but knew that it was the same direction that the Khmer Rouge soldiers had fled to, so they headed in the opposite direction. They were hoping they could make it to Phnom Penh. Certainly nothing could be as bad as the Khmer Rouge, they reasoned. Eventually hundreds of thousands, if not millions would flee Cambodia to escape the Khmer Rouge and the Vietnamese, crossing into border camps in Thailand. Noit and her remaining family members, however, continued to walk toward Phnom Penh to look for more of their family who might be alive.

For two months Noit and her family walked and slept along the road, reaching only about half of the way to the capital city from where they had begun. With so little food and strength, they could make very little progress each day. The weary family found some wood from a damaged old bridge and also found a man who agreed to help them cut the wood to make two simple wheels and a small cart to be pulled by their cow. The man only promised to help them if they would give them their other cow. They felt obligated and gave their other cow to him. The wheels were just one solid block of wood and there were no nails or wire to help put the cart together. Finally the rickety cart was completed. They placed their bit of rice and other foods they had gathered along the way onto the cart and continued in the direction of Phnom Penh. It was hard traveling so far with the lack of sustenance. Soon, however, the solid wood wheel wore through causing the rickety cart to rock and shake violently. Eventually it became unusable so they discarded it along the road.

Their journey continued, but they still had a great distance to travel to their old home. The heat, the hunger, and the walking became too much. They had made it to Kompong Chhnang province, but they were still nearly 90 km (55 miles) from home. Short of Phnom Penh they could go no further. There was no food, and no energy remaining to lift one foot in front of the other for Noit and her family.

Noit's mother was determined to keep her children alive, and return to the life she dreamed would be theirs again back at their old home in Phnom Penh. She searched for a way out of their tragic situation. She came upon a man who had found an abandoned military truck. The man was able to get it running and agreed to take Noit and her family to Phnom Penh for the price of their last cow. The truck, like the one that had taken them into the labor camps, soon was packed with other people who also paid an equally high price for their ride to the city. Once again Noit stood in the back of the truck, this time a little bit taller than during her first ride. Assumedly the other exhausted and starving passengers had also given up anything the man demanded for a standing position on the truck.

Everyone was disappointed when the man stopped several miles from the city, telling the people to get off because he would go no further. He was afraid of what the Vietnamese would do to him if he pulled into the city in an army truck. Although hungry and weak, with the realization they may soon reach home Noit and her family began walking again. They eventually got sight of the mighty Mekong River and entered Phnom Penh. They were shocked at the sight of their city. It had not been safeguarded. As people had reentered the city they took up residence in any livable structure. The once bustling capital which hosted as many as three million people now looked like a run-down ghost town. As they walked from the outskirts it was as if no one had survived. House after house was partially destroyed and there were no people.

Walking down familiar boulevards they were surprised to see weeds and even small trees growing in the streets. The buildings had no color, only a black mold covered each home from the harsh tropical weather. Doors and windows were open, sometimes completely missing. Many buildings were just rubble and sometimes Noit could not even remember what used to be at that site. The rusted remains of old vehicles and motorcycles sat unusable, still parked along the roads just as the day they left the city more than four years earlier.

Finally, they found their street and walked down the road toward their old house, not knowing what to expect as to its condition, though they were all hoping it had been miraculously spared. Upon walking up to their old home in the city they found their house was already occupied and the new residents would not relocate, so they just moved on and found another vacant place. Not knowing who the new occupiers were, they discerned there was no reason for any confrontation. They briefly stood outside for a moment and then continued walking. They stopped one night in an abandoned building near the weathered Independence Monument. They decided to keep moving and search for any of their relatives whose fates were still unknown.

Though they were back in the city, life was hard. They returned to a city which had been completely destroyed and abandoned for years. Roofs were rotten and falling in on themselves. There was no water, no electricity and no semblance of law and order.

As people came back in the city, they were desperate for everything. They needed firewood for cooking, but they had no axes or saws. People would go house to house looking for anything of value. Doors, windows, nails, floor tiles, and roof tiles were scavenged for use. Even the steel rebar was cut out of buildings, melted down and crude axes made from the metal. Light fixtures were long gone and of no use without electricity, so electric wires were ripped from all the buildings for the copper to sell and repurpose. The Khmer Rouge had removed most of the furniture and appliances out of homes and dumped them into the Mekong River. Returning to a city of this condition made life very hard and having to scavenge for everything only made it worse.

After a few days of wandering around looking for any familiar face, Noit's mother found a sister-in-law who had survived the torturous years of suffering. She had occupied an empty house, and welcomed Noit and her family to stay with her. One day, rummaging through abandoned buildings Noit found an old steel-framed bed and she hauled it back to her house. She had no mattress, but her mother made her a little mat from grasses and placed that over the protruding steel springs so she could have a bed to sleep on. That would be her bed for more than two decades. The old steel bed is still in our house today.

If I were an artist I would draw you a picture, but try to think how Noit and her family, and others like her, walked home:

Swollen heads from malnutrition.

Emaciated bodies.

A 16 year old, Noit, weighing only 20 kilos (45 pounds).

Her mother weighed 25 kilos (52 pounds). She died soon after their walk back to Phnom Penh.

Walking slowly; faces to the ground.

Only walking 1-3 kilometers was possible in an entire day due to their lack of strength.

No water to drink. Noit would drink muddy water from any source, like buffalo wallows.

Temperatures between 95 and 110 degrees (32-43 Celsius) during April 1979.

Khmer Rouge would ambush those walking.

Vietnamese shooting over the heads of those walking with machine guns and nearby artillery firing at the hiding Khmer Rouge forces.

Fear in every step.

Dead bodies decomposing along the road; those who never made it home.

Walkers would attack suspected Khmer Rouge soldiers trying to hide in the population. All suspected Khmer Rouge were hacked to death in mob justice.

Landmines covered every road side. They would have to sleep on the dirt road, because if they stepped off they might get killed.

Bushes had few leaves, because that is all the people had to eat.

Quiet for hours on end. People isolated themselves from each other while walking.

The smell of decomposing bodies everywhere.

Hopelessness.

Every town and village destroyed, the Khmer Rouge literally destroyed every population center.

Bridges blown out or burning from Khmer Rouge ambushes to stop the advancing Vietnamese and Cambodian army.

Most victims never made it home, but just stayed somewhere along the road, making a random home for themselves among people they did not know. Hoping, just maybe, one of their dozens of relatives, siblings or family members made it out alive. Even after thirty years reunions are rare.

Noit and her remaining family members walked 150 kilometers (95 miles) from the border of *Battambang* province to *Kompong Chhnang* town. In her condition, it took her two months. There, she traded a cow that she had found for a ride to Phnom Penh the last 90 kilometers (55 miles). When she arrived at her home, it was occupied by another family who made it back before her. Noit, her mother, sister and brother then occupied another empty home. They still had no food to eat. They walked to the Mekong River to drink water and they hoped to see other family members come walking back into the city like they did. But, they never did return. They even held out hope for a few years. But the reality is that their bodies are scattered among the rice fields of *Pursat* Province, Cambodia - a long, long walk away.

Part Two: New Life

A Heroic Cambodian Mother

Chapter ជំពូកទី ១២ **12**

Noit's mother, Hieng Hun, was quite a typical Cambodian mother. Nearly everyone in Cambodia might describe their mother with the same few adjectives: Faithful, selfless, resourceful. These words describe Noit's mother perfectly.

Hieng was born into a time when it was easy to identify a mother by her traditional roles. No Cambodian woman had ever graduated from high school by the 1930's when she was born. Girls would spend only a few years going to school, which was more like a day care center, until they were old enough to help in the home and learn how to be good future mothers. Few women could read. Noit's mother was also illiterate. Reading, it was presumed, would allow women to be able to flirt secretly with boys. To preserve their virtue, women were not allowed to read. They only had to exist. They were never to draw attention to themselves. They should always keep themselves covered so they could remain as fair skinned as possible. A daughter is a good family asset if she is lighter in complexion and cute looking. With such qualities she would be able to marry into a good family. Outward beauty is everything in a culture which does not have courtship.

When Noit's mother was young, a young man came to speak to her parents. He was studying to be a teacher which was a very respectable position. If he was from a farming family, the family would likely not have approved of their marriage. The young man, Then Thuon, would likely be able to provide well for the family. Few questions were asked, but the engagement was more a negotiation. The groom's family negotiated for the bride price (called "*tly tuk dah*" or "nursing fee" in Cambodian). They made an agreement and quickly they were married. Soon Hieng was pregnant with her first child. Then, as is often the case with Cambodian husbands, Thuon quit coming to the house each day. No one talked openly about it, but everyone knew that he had other women. In fact, they would discover that he had other whole families. Unfortunately, this has been a very acceptable part of the Cambodian culture. At one point they discovered that Then Thuon may have had as many as seven wives. Noit grew up knowing her father more from a few pictures on the wall because she rarely saw him in person. When he would come to spend the night with his wife, Hieng would always greet him, make him his favorite food and slip into the bedroom with him after the kids went to sleep. After a day or so he would be gone for months on end. Noit never heard her mother say anything negative about her dad, only that he never provided anything. Hieng would constantly work hard to sell a few things to make ends meet and provide for her children which grew to seven, including a boy that she adopted.

Even when the Khmer Rouge took over Phnom Penh, Noit's father was with another wife and so she was never able to see her father again. It was only later, after they returned to Phnom Penh that they found one of the other wives and she knew his fate. She explained that when the Khmer Rouge took over, the Khmer Rouge asked young students to identify their teachers. They reasoned with the students saying that their teachers had taught them foreign lies and were traitors to the Khmer culture. A student had pointed out Then Thuon to the Khmer Rouge and he was quickly shot. It was only the first or second day that the Khmer Rouge had come into Phnom Penh. His body was dumped in some side alley in Phnom Penh.

Hieng was not an outspoken mother, like a proper Cambodian mother. She just quietly provided for her children the best she could. Even when they were separated during the Khmer Rouge she would find a way to sneak away and get close to her children, though she could not provide any affection, for fear of being killed. When her children died, she kept her pain internally and never showed her distress outwardly. Though her body was completely broken during the Khmer Rouge captivity, she struggled with every bit of energy she could muster to get her children back home. When their home was lost to someone else, she determined to make a new one.

She was the perfect Cambodian mother. Faithful to the end, though she was not given faithfulness. She was selfless, always giving to her children and keeping nothing for herself. Though she was selfless, she was treated with selfishness. She was resourceful. She lost everything at the whim of young Khmer Rouge soldiers. Every possession was stolen. Her children were ripped from her and several died, but she found those who remained and kept them alive. When they were freed from the Khmer Rouge, though danger crouched around them, she successfully got her children to a new home and was able to see them have enough food to survive. Unfortunately, she was only able to see one child married. Noit's older sister, Than.

Than was about five years older than Noit and a beautiful young woman in her 20's at the end of the Khmer Rouge regime in 1979. Noit's mother was worried about her daughter. Being so beautiful with long black hair she was afraid her daughter would be forced to marry a soldier or even be raped by Vietnamese soldiers. When a young man, who had a job as a police officer in the new government, approached Hieng to ask about her daughter's hand, it was a quick agreement. Prum Phal, the young policeman, was poor and had no money to pay a bride price but he promised to offer one cow for the wedding celebration. Soon, Than was married in a simple wedding. Weddings that close to the liberation from the Khmer Rouge were very basic affairs. Phal arranged for Than to also get a job as a police officer and they were granted a house by the Vietnamese government in central Phnom Penh by the New Market as a benefit. The entire family moved into the crumbling little house.

Noit's mother was the perfect Cambodian mother. She survived and was able to help three of her children survive too. Yet, it broke her. Even after they returned to Phnom Penh, and re-established their home, she never regained her strength. She remained weak and frail. There was almost no medical care available. Eventually, she could hardly move and was in constant pain. The surviving children gathered up some money to take her to a doctor. The doctor said she had cancer, but there was no proper testing or even any treatment available for her. He recommended just to take her home. Noit spent every day by her mother's side. She had learned the important characteristics of a Cambodian wife: to be faithful, selfless and resourceful. She would rub her mothers sore legs, and rub her body with a cool cloth. She would feed her soft rice porridge little spoonful by spoonful. The Khmer Rouge oppression had broken her body too much. Maybe in a different time she could have been helped, but not in Vietnamese occupied Phnom Penh.

One morning, Hieng gave her last gasp of air and she faded into eternity. Noit sat by her side and cried, holding her mothers lifeless body. The only person who ever loved her was gone. She was truly a heroic Cambodian mother.

Vietnamese occupation was nearly as arduous as the Khmer Rouge. Spies were everywhere as the Vietnamese mistrusted their Cambodian counterparts. They could not tell who was loyal to the Vietnamese army and who were still willing to fight with the Khmer Rouge. The war was still going on, though it had moved out of most urban areas which were firmly in Vietnamese control. The roads and villages connecting the government controlled areas were a different story. Ambushes were frequent, bombings common and a new form of warfare emerged: a cowards war. Indiscriminately placing landmines everywhere in the fields, roads, and any pathway became the common strategy. The Chinese were supplying the Khmer Rogue with thousands of cheap mines and their jungle patrols would plant them anywhere they felt an adversary might walk. After more than a decade of jungle fighting, it is estimated that more than ten million mines were planted leaving Cambodia one of the most deadly places to live on earth. Still decades later, the threat of being blown up by a mine is very real. While half of the Cambodian population today was born after the Khmer Rouge reign, the people still suffer the effects of this cowards war.

After Noit's mother died, Noit needed a job to support herself. Noit's sister was able to get a job for her at the police department also. Now they had become a police family. Hoping to get Noit a good and safe position, she applied for a job with the traffic police. In those days there were fewer than a thousand cars remaining in Cambodia. Most people walked or rode bicycles, with a few motorcycles. There was little for the traffic police to do. There were no traffic signal lights, so at a few major intersections they would have a wood platform in the center of the road when for a few hours out of each day, the traffic police stood to direct traffic of bicycles, motorcycles and the occasional official car. At just the sight of the uniform (which closely resembled the Vietnamese military uniform) an approaching bicycle or motorcycle would freeze in its tracks. The police were respected because they had the authority to bring stiff penalties on the people.

Noit only worked in order to survive. She hated ever being the center of attention standing on that block in the center of the road. Being there, and her lack of anonymity, caused her a great deal of stress. Subconsciously, she felt as if something bad would happen to her there. Whenever possible, she would talk her way out of the traffic direction duties, and she longed for a desk job. She would much rather stay in the office doing paperwork. It seemed much

safer. So, eventually, she was assigned to take care of the recording of all of the officers salaries. Quickly, she was known by everyone as the quiet young policewoman in the office. They knew her by her legal name "Nimol", and to this day are the only people who call her that. Amazingly, out of the six hundred officers in the capital city, only six were women. In a country with no concept of sexual harassment laws or a moral standard to prevent abuse, it was a huge challenge to work among all those men. She continually reminded herself that she was only working there to survive.

Noit's salary was just enough to survive. She was paid about $20 in cash and given a sack of rice per month. The rice seemed to be the more valuable benefit because usually she would have to wait months for her salary to be paid to her. While she was a police officer and still young the government started high school classes on the weekends so more young people could get an education, but still be employed. Noit was able to complete high school this way, while still working full-time with the police department. Noit stayed with her sister and brother-in-law at the police-provided house so she only kept a bit of her money and gave the rest to her sister.

Noit had no hope in her job. She had no hope in her country and with the rest of her family lost forever to the genocide she saw no reason to live. At the completion of each day she would return home and wish that she could just fast-forward her life to the end and be done with it all. A coworker shared with her that she found a tablet that would help her sleep and not have constant nightmares about the horrific conditions she had lived through. Noit started taking the sleeping pills and sure enough she could make it through the night. Soon, she advanced to taking the pills whenever she wasn't working. Having been overcome by hopelessness she hoped she could sleep through life. She existed in this hopeless state for nearly a decade. Her work never changed, nor did the condition of her broken country.

All media in the country was completely restricted under the communist government so the Cambodian people were still living like a frog in a well, because they didn't know about anything that was happening in the world. The only political relationships that Cambodia had were with communist countries like Vietnam, China, Yugoslavia, Poland, Russia, Cuba, North Korea and other Soviet-satellite bloc countries.   Noit's younger brother, who studied painting in school was given a scholarship to study art in Poland. There he immersed himself in classical European painting techniques, but communication was quite difficult back to Cambodia and he was never able to come to visit.   Only once a year or so he was able to call and   talk to his sisters back in Phnom Penh. Those memories of hearing from their young brother were sweet, though the times of talking to him were very brief.

In 1991 the Soviet Union began to unravel. Though they had no international news, they could see that the Soviets were leaving Cambodia in droves. At one time there were more than 5,000 advisors attached to the embassy in several massive compounds. Now, they appeared to be mostly empty. Once again, the people felt as if the world cared nothing about their plight.   The international community did not rescue them from the Khmer Rouge. They were invaded by their longtime enemy Vietnam. They had heard rumors that those who had escaped to Thailand were also being mistreated and many were killed in forceful military repatriations back into Khmer Rouge controlled areas.   Now, the few foreigners who seemed to want to help Cambodia were leaving too. However, unknown to her something else was about to happen. Those who knew the larger political situation were looking for a way to save Cambodia.   In 1991 and 1992 they saw what was to happen: foreign military with white planes, white vehicles and many foreign people began arriving in Cambodia. They were a UN Peacekeeping force called "UNTAC".

Soon, there were non-communist nations being represented in Cambodia. Westerners had been absent for nearly two decades but now they were regularly coming to Cambodia. The presence of French, Swiss, American and Singaporean people became more common on the streets of Cambodia. They all needed workers, but they needed English as a prerequisite for hiring. Under the communist government, the young people were only allowed to learn Russian or Vietnamese which was useless to the new foreigners. Soon, small English schools were popping up around Cambodia. Noit saw one called "Global Network". She started attending some classes. They had a strange style of teaching and often sang songs. One of the first "English" words she learned was "Hosanna!" After some time her Swiss teacher asked her if she would visit a church with them. This shocked her because she knew nothing of Christians. Her response was that she could not go because she was Buddhist. Sadly, the school asked her not to come back for English classes when she refused to go to church. However, God wasn't finished.

Noit's cousin had rented an apartment to a tall lanky Dutch girl who wanted to learn Khmer. Each evening Noit would go to her cousins house to try and learn some English from this lady named "Joke" (pronounced Yoka). Joke was a nurse attached with Youth With a Mission. She wanted to learn Khmer so she could share about Jesus. Noit and her cousin were her first targets!

Noit wasn't interested in Jesus, but she listened to learn English. She began to learn more about sin, evil and how Jesus could remove all these things from people's lives. In Buddhism this was impossible. They believed that everything bad which happened was because of a person's own sin and was their own fault. They call this *karma*. Each day Joke would talk to Noit and they became good friends.

One day, knowing the past genocide which Noit had survived, Joke told Noit that "if you believe in Jesus, he can be your new father." Joke knew that Noit had lost her father to the Khmer Rouge. Well, it had the opposite effect. Noit thought of her father who was always absent, was unfaithful to her mother and seemed to care nothing about the family and decided if Jesus was anything like her father, she didn't want him.

One day Joke gave Noit a passage of scripture to read. Noit read these words from the Bible, *"But the fruit of the Spirit is love, joy, peace, patience, kindness, goodness, faithfulness, gentleness and self-control"* (Galatians 5:22-23). After she read this, stopping to pause on each word, it was as if these words were completely foreign to her life. Then Joke said, "You can have *hope* that you will see in your life!

Noit was puzzled. Hope. Hope. Noit thought, "I have no hope." The Holy Spirit used that word and just kept burning into her heart. For days she kept hearing that word echo in her heart, "hope, hope, hope." Noit desperately wanted hope. Her life was completely hopeless.

One day, it all made sense in her mind and her heart was happy. She desired this hope from Jesus. She told Joke, "I want to believe in Jesus now." Joke prayed with her to accept Jesus into her heart. Finally, she had hope in her heart.

Believing in Jesus was something very new for Noit. Her entire life she did not know anything about Jesus. She didn't know any Bible stories. She never heard of Adam, Abraham or Moses and had never heard of Israel. The only thing she new about Jesus was that apparently he was French!

Noit was excited with her new faith and she wanted to share Jesus with her sister and cousin. However, the response she got was cold. Her cousin didn't want to talk to her anymore. Her sister and brother-in-law were angry and said that she was betraying her country. Noit would often work and then go to study in the evening, missing dinner time. Her sister used to keep a plate of food for her in the evening when she returned late from studies or work, but now they told her that, "if you want to eat, you should get your food from Jesus!" The rejection hurt her badly, but she knew Jesus was true. Noit had so much pain in her heart though.

One day, after believing in Jesus, she started crying. Noit cried for hours and hours and couldn't control herself. After she finished, she felt different. It was as if the Holy Spirit used her tears to cleanse her heart, the pain, the disappointment, the fear, the horrible memories, they all left. Something new was in her heart. She had hope.

You didn't survive the Khmer Rouge by being friendly with others, and helping others get through the torturous days. Self-preservation with divine assistance was really the only way to survive. Those who stood out were quickly cut off. After Noit arrived back in Phnom Penh each person had to forage for their survival and create their own opportunities. Stealing, deception and treachery were common. Also, a self-preserving ingenuity was born. After having survived the Khmer Rouge, it seems as though when the threat of people actively trying to kill you was not there, it was easier to survive by scrounging for essentials, bartering for what was needed and rebuilding their lives with little resources. The government was now ruled by a military government and the civil war would continue for decades to come. There was nothing easy about life under military rule. The desperation of the Khmer Rouge captivity was over, but there was still nothing to look forward too.

However, after more than a decade of military rule, a change happened in Noit when she learned of the gospel of Jesus. The teachings of Jesus were diametrically opposed to everything she had ever been previously taught. God gave her a new heart and new focus. Rather than dwelling on the difficulties of her life, she decided that she would use her life to help others so that they would never have to endure the pain which she had to survive. Jesus' teaching of putting others before self opposes every cultural norm. A decade earlier it would have been unlikely that this new foreign message would be received in Cambodia. Indeed, Christians have been actively trying to evangelize this isolated Buddhist nation since 1555 with little fruit to show. However, the social genocide in which Khmer Buddhists were killing their own people shattered the dominance of the religion. Jesus transformed Noit's life.

As a young Christian she began to explore the reality of her new God, Jesus. She understood that Jesus was real and all she needed to do was talk to him and he would hear her and answer her prayers. So she decided to test out this new Jesus. She secretly asked him if he could help her. Late at night when no one could hear her she whispered, "Jesus, if you are real, please help me get a good job. One that has a good salary and good coworkers so that I can help my sister and my family more."

A few days later, Joke told her that a friend of hers named Bob was looking for tellers in his new Singaporean bank. Noit applied. Unbeknownst to Noit, Bob had asked Joke about Noit as a reference. Joke told Bob, "If you're looking for someone who understands banking then Noit would not be good, however, if you can teach her, Noit has the highest integrity, she is loyal and will work very hard." She was hired. Noit immediately knew that this "foreign" Jesus was indeed real. Jesus was alive and cared about her.

The word "hope" has an important meaning for Noit since she has become a Christian. Before, when she was listening to those present the gospel, she often heard the word "hope". It puzzled her. "What was hope?" She would say to herself. She just existed. She could not fathom "hope". She couldn't imagine that there was anything more to life, much less any purpose or value.

Her Dutch friend Joke gave her a Bible and told her to read it. Noit began spending hours upon hours reading her precious Bible. In those days, the early days of the new freedom for the isolated church, Bibles were difficult to come by. At night Noit would read chapter after chapter and continued book by book. She was amazed by the stories, which were completely foreign to her. She never heard of strange names like Moses and Abraham, much less ever heard of kings named David and Solomon. Ancient Cambodian kings with names like Suryavarman and Jayavarman VII were household names to her. Then she read a verse which shot out from the pages and penetrated her heart. As she read in Jeremiah she read the words, "'For I know the plans I have for you,' declares the Lord, 'plans to prosper you and not to harm you, plans to give you hope and a future'" (Jeremiah 29:11, NIV). When she read that verse, something jumped in her heart. Life came back into her and stirred in her a sense of purpose. God has a plan for her! God would give her hope and a future! This was great news! Suddenly, the life that was destroyed by the Khmer Rouge had been sparked back inside of her.

She learned about Jesus, and how he was killed. Betrayed by his disciple, his friend. Murdered by his own people and tortured on the cross until dead. She could relate. She saw this same brutality in her nation. Yet, Jesus was different. He said to forgive. He loved those who hated him and killed him. It brought Jesus peace. She reckoned it would bring her peace as well. She asked Jesus to help her to forgive those who destroyed her family and traumatized her life. She didn't know if Jesus was doing it, but she didn't feel any hatred. She felt clean in her heart. The sadness though, was still very heavy.

Excited with this new faith in Jesus she started sharing with as many people as possible. She shared her faith with her sister, but her response was disgust. She shared with her police coworkers, but their response was to be suspicious of her and suspect her of being treasonous to her national culture. Some would listen, but ask challenging questions to try and understand Christianity. It was difficult for her to answer their questions. Many of her friends would question her faith, based on false rumors about Christians. They would ask things like,

"Is it true, to believe in Jesus you have to kick over a statue of Buddha?" or,

"Why do Christians celebrate and are happy when their parents die?" followed by a similar question,

"What would your parents think of Jesus' teaching that you should *not* obey your parents?"

Others, would be more pragmatic and recommend to her,

"When you are around your foreign friends it's okay to be a Christian, but around Cambodians you can still be Buddhist. That way you can have two religions and be 50/50."

These cultural misconceptions and the environment in which less than 0.01% of Cambodian were Christians would be a big challenge for her, but also spur her on toward studying and understanding her own faith through the Bible.

The Khmer Rouge and the effects of the genocide had created a society where there was constant mistrust. No one knew who was a spy or who was a friend. Mistrust led to a break in relationships nationwide. Families were destroyed and relationships between mother and father, and parents and children were broken. The Khmer Rouge would forcibly marry young people against their will, and others married out of fear of being abused. While young families began having babies, there were key elements of family life which were often missing. Love and affection were rare. Noit was living in a broken family and she was seeing the families around her face the same situations.

Her family owned a little plot of land across the river. Many poor families were living there. On the weekends she went across the river with Joke to rest from the weeks activities. Joke would play her guitar and they would worship the Lord together. However, it was never very restful, as soon as Joke would begin playing the guitar little kids would scamper out of their little homes to find where the music was coming from. They would peek in the windows or just walk right in the room. So, Joke and Noit decided they would begin teaching the children songs and about Jesus. Noit wanted so much that these children would be able to have a real childhood and be free from the pain she had gone though. However, the poverty around the children limited their potential. Noit had such a burden for them. Over time, the restful weekends turned into a full church, which still meets on her family's property. Noit eventually quit her job as a police officer and joined with Joke to lead a ministry called "Hope for Cambodia's Children". The ministry would later employ nearly two hundred staff. Their target was to minister to children in impoverished slums. Each week, they helped over 30,000

children. Thousands would come to Christ and hundreds of new churches were planted across poor communities in Cambodia.

Yet, even as Noit grew in her faith, she sometimes still struggled with unanswered questions in her life. She wondered if there would ever be justice. Would anything lost ever be restored? Years of living in fear and being traumatized had caused her to withdrawn in her emotions. Noit concealed her deepest thoughts where no one could find them. The whole society she lived in was identified by lying and deception. Violent crime were still common, yet people would respond with indifference, hoping to avoid any conflict. Though her community had so many poor and destitute people, no one would help others. People would just look out for themselves. All these behaviors were engrained in them from the oppressive Khmer Rouge regime.

But Noit wondered, could others find the same hope that she had found? Could she help them to find hope and purpose in their lives? As she lived her new Christian life, led children to Christ, and began to disciple young believers, Noit yearned that they too would know Jesus and the hope that he brings. She had faith that the promises of God are true and that, in God's timing, he would indeed work everything in her life for good.

As Noit matured in the Lord, a special passage of scripture that led to a new life in Christ helped to pattern her Christian life. She yearned to understand, live out and help others to have the same life she had. . . Fruit of the spirit.

"But the fruit of the Spirit is love, joy, peace, forbearance, kindness, goodness, faithfulness, gentleness and self-control. Against such things there is no law" (Galatians 5:22-23, NIV).

Here was the definition of a Christian life. Noit saw everything she desired for the culture of Cambodia represented in this verse. It became Noit's passion to live these characteristics of a Spirit-filled life with all her being.

While bombs were falling on Cambodia, a little boy was playing in the corn fields of Iowa, completely isolated from any danger. When Noit was forced into slavery, digging water canals, planting rice and collecting cow manure for fertilizer, Steve was an aspiring Boy Scout who would earn merit badges in practical skills that he might never use in the future. While Noit, at sixteen years of age, worked to survive with nearly her entire family being deceased, Steve was playing every sport available, volunteering in small projects for community development during free time from school, and was surrounded every moment by a loving family.

During a university exchange program which sent Steve to Uzbekistan, God called him to a life of service outside of America's comfortable borders. As soon as Steve graduated from college, the first opportunity that came to him was serving in Cambodia, a country which only recently had its first democratic election. This was the first time, since 1975, the nation was allowing foreigners in, though the civil war was still ongoing.

In 1994 Steve arrived in Cambodia, the year Steve and Noit first met. At that time there were less than a dozen churches in Cambodia. Steve attended one called "Open Gate Church". Noit, being a new Christian, also attended this church. It was one of the few churches that was not an "underground church", though there were no sign boards highlighting their location. However, it seemed the authorities allowed it to exist. Though the two met at church, Noit spoke little English at the time and Steve likewise spoke almost no Cambodian.

Their paths soon crossed again when Noit worked for a banking startup called "Singapore Bank". The manager of the bank was a Christian and a friend of Steve's. As Steve spent time at the bank with his friend, seeing Noit provided another way to engage in conversation.

The third time Steve and Noit's paths would intersect was more significant. Steve was working with a Baptist short-term mission and was looking to change. World Relief had contacted Steve about working with a new child evangelism program. They had asked Steve to start churches in the areas where they were working with the child evangelism program. It seemed like a great fit. Noit was the Cambodian director of the ministry and Steve was training church planters. Their friendship grew as they worked together daily for two years. Steve and Noit were engaged in the summer of 1998 and prepared for a future wedding.

The couple thought they should ask a pastor to help counsel them, since Noit was an orphan, and Steve lived half-way around the world from his family. They went to the most respected pastor they knew, Pastor Heng Cheng, and asked for his teaching and counsel for their lives. Pastor Cheng spoke many things to them, but one word of counsel stood out. He told them, "God has called you to a national ministry. Because you will be national leaders, you will have to travel. Since you will have to travel, you will often have to be apart. So, from now until your wedding, do not talk to each other in person or on the phone. Learn to be apart. You will have your whole life to be together." Steve was a bit dumbfounded. He asked for clarification. Sure enough, Steve had understood the instructions correctly. This certainly went against Steve's entire culture. In the West, there is a culture of dating and courting. Not in Cambodia. Once a person meets someone they like, and that individual confirms that they in turn like the other, it's a done deal. Waiting to be married seemed like the longest seven months in Steve's life.

Steve cleverly discovered a way to see Noit during those waiting months. Steve knew that Noit drove her little motorcycle scooter every Saturday from her house to the church where she taught a Bible study. On that day, Steve waited on the corner near Noit's house, "coincidentally" riding his motorcycle next to Noit for the few miles it took to get to the church. They would chat about the week as they rode side-by-side down the road. That would be Steve's weekly contact with Noit! One Saturday morning as Steve headed to the "coincidental" rendezvous point his rear tire went flat. He panicked! He couldn't possibly miss his one interaction with Noit during the week because of a flat tire. So, Steve decided to sacrifice the tire. He saw Noit coming his direction and he pulled up alongside her. Steve's motorcycle was jerking violently, making it necessary to grip the handlebars tightly to keep from falling. Every few seconds, people would gesture to him to pull over because the tire was flat. Steve was too enthralled with Noit to stop. After riding the few miles Steve said goodbye to Noit and proceeded immediately to find a place where he could replace his shredded tire and damaged rim!

Steve and Noit both wanted to have a Christian ceremony that reflected the Cambodian culture. Most "Christian" weddings were simply a copy of an American wedding that had little meaning in the Cambodian culture. A Cambodian wedding entailed respecting the parents, honoring some strange traditions, but they desired to center the service around Jesus Christ instead of cultural tradition. In a Cambodian wedding, the bride and groom become as king and queen for a day with all its pomp and circumstance. That meant forgoing a white wedding dress, as white is the Cambodian color of death, worn during funerals. Steve would also have to walk in a procession down a main thoroughfare to the wedding hall, wearing something similar to a giant golden diaper! The wedding festivities would last as entire day. After months of incredible patience, Steve and Noit were married March 6, 1999. Thanks to the help of several pastors, Steve and

Noit had a beautiful beginning to their new life together.

Soon afterward, both their ministries began to grow and expand, reaching every corner of the nation. Shortly after Steve and Noit were married they met a New Zealand pastor who prophesied to Noit, "God will restore everything you have lost and give you even more." Those words pierced her heart and she knew that they were the promises of God being spoken to her. It seemed impossible, but she knew that Jesus loves to do what others see as impossible.

During the next two decades Steve and Noit's family and ministry continued to grow. They quickly ramped up their discipleship training program and invited pastors from all over Cambodia to attend a seminar in Phnom Penh. In those days, with no internet and very limited cell phone coverage, the only way to get information out was by word-of-mouth. The day before the seminar, only seven people had pre-registered, but Steve and Noit decided to proceed with the training no matter how many attended. On the day of the seminar, pastors started showing up from places throughout the nation. Over 170 church leaders attended from around Cambodia, giving birth to *Antioch Institute* which today has reached every province and every district of Cambodia with discipleship teaching, leadership training and theological courses. Today, a large percentage of all Cambodian Christian leaders, regardless of denomination or affiliation, have received their theological training from *Antioch Institute.*

Most of the church leaders of Cambodia are rural, poor and involved in subsistence farming. Most of the urban pastors grew up in the same situation, simply moving to the city for a more convenient lifestyle or in pursuit of advanced education.

One day, Noit and Steve were in a jungle clearing in eastern Cambodia visiting one of their students. The student and his wife had been former Khmer Rouge soldiers. When they had heard the gospel of Jesus, they had repented of their past and believed in him. Their hearts were transformed, but they were still trapped in dire poverty. Walking through a corn field cut into a small jungle clearing, being led by their two youngest daughters, Noit and Steve saw the potential of these little kids. Yet they had no chance to be educated. There was not a school within hours of their home. Noit and Steve's hearts burned for these children who had no opportunity for a different life outside the jungle. Within a few months, after buying a small piece of property on a hillside in Kracheh province, *Imparting Smiles Children's Home* was born. There were thirteen children, including the two girls Noit and Steve met in the cornfield. Since the start of *Imparting Smiles*, more than three hundred children, including children of church leaders, orphaned and abandoned, trafficked and sexually abused children have been able to benefit from two wonderful homes. Dozens have gone to universities and been able to obtain good jobs to provide for their families. Many have studied abroad, taking up ministry or teaching full-time, to help others break free from poverty as well. Some of the children from remote jungles, whose parents have spent their entire lives isolated in the jungle, have even studied abroad!

A few years later, Steve met a minister who asked him about the largest and most silent unreached people group in the world. Steve, who considered himself well-studied, was perplexed. The minister spoke about abortion and the millions of babies who perish every year, and have no voice. Steve's response to the man was like many Protestant ministers saying that "surely, Christian women would not abort their babies." The minister assured Steve that throughout the world, the sanctity of life was not honored among Christians and it was a topic which Protestants largely ignored. Over the next few days, as the conversation churned in their hearts, Steve and Noit coincidentally/divinely met several pastors' wives who indeed had aborted their babies, or were seeking to abort their babies. Steve and Noit discovered that among Protestants, the sanctity of life was not taught and abortion was widespread, just as it was among the Buddhist population. In Cambodia, abortion providers have saturated the country, offering free and low-cost abortions with few limits. These providers have deceived women, telling them that abortion is just another form of contraception to remove unwanted bloody tissue. After praying and seeking an approach to promote the sanctity of life, Steve and Noit formed the *Hope Center* in northwestern Cambodia assisting women who felt the need to abort their babies. The center, with its training, is also used to empower women who are often the most marginalized in society. After only three years, nearly one thousand babies have been saved from abortion. Hundreds of women have come to Christ. Dozens of new churches have been started in places where the women live, who initially were seeking to abort their precious babies. These churches have become centers of hope to other women in the area.

As more children were educated through Steve and Noit's ministry, the more intimately they became involved in the government educational system. At times they tried to support government teachers and schools to provide better education. Ultimately they realized they needed to start their own Christian schools if they were to truly make a difference in the educational opportunities available. *Antioch School* was born when they were contacted by a local private school that was going bankrupt in the capital city of Phnom Penh. Steve and Noit bought the assets and licensing of the school, changing its name to *Antioch School*. The name "Antioch" is special to Steve and Noit because it was there that the Apostle Paul was launched into missions, and it was a city which bordered eastern and western hemispheres. It seemed the methodology for Christian education, in a majority Buddhist country, would have to be a blend of eastern and western ideas, without compromising scripture and the gospel of Jesus. Having little background in Christian education, Steve pursued a Doctorate of Christian Education so that he could best lead and develop these new schools. There are currently two schools with more than five hundred students and a third school is being built as this book is being written. Talented Christian educators from Singapore and Australia have helped in training the teachers. Amazingly, most of the teachers are those children who have grown up in *Imparting Smiles,* and want to make a difference for the next generation.

Through the initial ministry called *Words of Life*, Steve and Noit have published hundreds of books related to Christian leadership; including discipleship, evangelistic and theological materials. They have produced millions of books over the last twenty years. Through their writing and translation efforts, they were often frustrated with the older Bible translations in Cambodian (Khmer). They often felt the word choices were quite archaic or inaccurate. Both pre-existing Bibles used obscure words and grammar which were a significant challenge for Cambodians to understand. In some ways they were like giving an old KJV Bible to a new Christian today. Both previous Bibles were translated from English and had primarily used foreigners to do the translation. As the *Words of Life* Cambodian team were praying about the possibility of taking on a new Bible translation, (translating the Bible from Greek and Hebrew into modern Cambodian), they were approached by the Asia Bible Society in Sendai, Japan. This group had also been praying about the need for a modern Bible translation in Cambodia and other nearby nations. The Cambodian team knew the task would be daunting. Prospective translators needed to attend theological schools overseas so they could be immersed in theology, interpretation, Biblical Greek and Biblical Hebrew. Upon graduation these translators returned to Cambodia and painstakingly began translating each word from Greek and Hebrew into Khmer. Along the way, they developed a Greek-Khmer lexicon with numerous Bible study helps, including an exhaustive concordance of the Bible. Many people are not aware that across the world, few languages other than English, German or French have Bible study helps. Most of the some six thousand languages with Bible translations have only the New Testament text. After more than two decades of work, the *Khmer Christian Bible* was completed and used across Cambodia, and will continue to be for generations to come.

Together, Steve and Noit continue to ask God for a bigger vision for Cambodia seeking to share the gospel into every corner and home in Cambodia. They know that building for the future is a key to the strength of this young first generation church. Steve and Noit seek to do everything with excellence and with a long-term perspective focusing on empowering Cambodians.

Chapter 17
ជំពូកទី ១៧

While looking back at the victories, it would be amiss not to mention the difficulties which Steve and Noit have faced each day. Cambodia, in the early 1990's, was not as open to the gospel as it seems now. While the national constitution provided for freedom of religious belief for all citizens, many local leaders didn't accept that Cambodian citizens would ever be anything but Buddhist. Early converts to Christianity were ostracized from their communities; many were shunned from their families and fired from places of employment, simply for professing to believe in Jesus Christ. Congregations, mostly formed in homes, worshipped quietly and in fear of local authorities.

Not only that, but in the early 1990's, the fighting with the Khmer Rouge had become somewhat of a stalemate. Throughout the years, ambushes could happen at any time and at any location. Most people carried weapons, and shootouts were common, even in the city. Political parties had their own armies which were loyal to them. During the yearly dry season, large scale fighting would commence against the Khmer Rouge, but because of the Khmer Rouge's heavily forested positions in the mountainous border areas, the war had been a stalemate for over a decade. As soon as the daily monsoon rains came, tanks and artillery bogged down in the mud making forward movement impossible. The two major political parties had amassed forces around the capital city. It was rumored that politicians were courting the Khmer Rouge to join either side. It all came to a head on the fifth of July, 1997, as tank battles and street skirmishes broke out around the capital city. Families who had survived the past genocide were petrified that the Khmer Rouge would return. People fled the city by the thousands, just trying to get away.

Foreigners began looking for the fastest way out of the country and were taking refuge in one of the riverside hotels where embassies were also setting up command posts. Steve, living alone in a wood house, feared his house would be burned down by incendiary rounds flying overhead and rockets exploding in his neighborhood. He opted to flee to Noit's concrete block house where she was holed up with a mission team visiting from Singapore; a short-term trip they would never forget.

After waiting out the fighting, Steve was required by his organization to flee Cambodia along with most other foreigners. Within a few weeks, as the victor became clear, Steve returned to Cambodia. Many foreigners quickly fled the country, after claiming they were willing to "give their lives" for Cambodia. Cambodian pastors felt dejected by the actions of those who said that they loved them. Steve vowed never to flee any situation like that again. After Steve and Noit married, they made contingency plans which involved staying in Cambodia when military conflict arose.

Another tragedy occurred with Sit, Noit's only living younger brother, who was given a scholarship to study art in Poland. Sit left Cambodia in1991 to study painting, but it was hard for him to communicate with his sisters back home. In 1997 when he heard of the fighting in Phnom Penh, he tried to call Cambodia but there was no answer. All communications into the country had been cut off. Still suffering from post-traumatic stress from the Khmer Rouge he feared the worst; the last of his family being killed. It unnerved him and he became unstable. Soon after the fighting in Cambodia ceased, Noit had a visitor come to the office from the Polish Embassy. Somberly she was told that her brother's body was found floating in the Bay of Gdansk in Poland. Noit's only brother was gone too. The pain of such news was even greater than the previous deaths, because of how miraculous it had been that they had survived the genocide. It seemed as though tragedy was always close to Noit's family.

Again and again, it seemed tragedy struck Noit. Noit's sister, Than, had four children. Since both Than, and her husband Phal, worked full-time jobs with the police, Noit cared for their four children from birth. Noit loved them as her own children. Pin, was the oldest, a girl. Pich, the oldest boy, was tough but cute. Do was a lanky smart boy who loved playing sports. Own, meaning "youngest" was the baby boy of the family. They were the pride and joy of the family. They were an aspiring new generation after the majority of their family had been lost under the Khmer Rouge.

During those days, in rainy season, the city flooded terribly. The city's septic system had not been updated since the war, and had been installed during the French colonial era over a century earlier. The city had only a few hundred thousand people at that time, unlike the bustling city of two million it has become. Noit's nephew, Do, a recent high school graduate and university student, was taking up art; the family tradition. It was a typical monsoonal day with afternoon rains drenching the city. It was as if sheets of water were being dumped onto the city each afternoon. The drains quickly clogged and the streets flooded with murky water. It was impossible to ride a bicycle or motorcycle as the flood waters were too high. Noit's nephew did what he had done many times before, wade through the floodwaters to his house. However, on this day, a mere two blocks from his house, Do was making his way down a flooded street, trying to avoid potholes and open sewers. He placed his hand on a light pole to stable himself as he waded through the near waist deep water. A bolt of electricity shot though him, instantly killing him. His smoking body floated down the street. Several people, seeing what had happened, ran away in panic, fearing they would be electrocuted as well. A foreigner rushed into the flooded street trying to save Do, but there was nothing he could do. Once again, a call came through to Noit with tragic news. Immediately, Steve and Noit got into their raised 4x4 vehicle to make their way to the family house. The waters nearly swamped the vehicle. As they drove, the floodwaters often covered the hood of the vehicle, but the Diesel engine didn't stall. Again, Noit had to suffer the pain of such a personal loss. The tragedy stung even worse, because his death was due to the incompetence of others and the poverty of the nation.

Steve and Noit continue to serve in ministry, traveling extensively, willingly going any place where people want them to share the gospel and train new leaders for the church. Not only have they faced their own tragedies, but they have also grieved in the tragedies of others. In only one of hundreds of examples, Pastor Doun and his wife, whom Steve and Noit loved dearly, had fifteen children. Nine of the children have died horrible deaths; from trees being felled on them, motor vehicle accidents or emergency illnesses when no medical care was available. Steve and Noit have grieved with parents such as these, have helped to bury children, and at times have held the bodies of dying friends as they suffered their last moments. With HIV and AIDS growing in the country, young people have regularly passed away, leaving their parents grieving and alone. Accidents, due to poverty and lack of regulation, have claimed many people as well. Electricians climb electric poles with no protection. Cars drive carelessly, without thought to the safety of others. In the early years, it was rare to see anyone wearing a helmet on a motorcycle, much less a bicycle. Many 'little' accidents would end in fatal head injuries. Steve and Noit have also known several pastors to be blinded or maimed when hitting landmines as they gardened around their homes. As ministers, Steve and Noit are often called to help families during these times of grieving. Their grief and trauma are painful for everyone.

However, one day, Steve and Noit received shocking news that they could never have imagined. Steve was about to begin preaching at one of their training conferences. His phone, one of his first cell phones, began ringing in his pocket. The lighted number showed 007, which in Cambodia signified an international call. It was unusual to receive an international call, so Steve stepped aside to answer the call. It was his mother. She had shocking news. She told Steve that his dad, who had been a missionary in the Philippines for thirty years, had been a victim of a terrorist bombing. Steve's mother and her mission organization had been trying to contact Steve. Steve's mother told him to pray, and then she needed to hang up. Steve rushed home to be with Noit, and wait for further news. Steve's dad and mom had chosen to live in restless Mindanao, a region of the Philippines where Muslims had been fighting for decades, if not centuries. Steve's dad was a teacher; a music teacher. He used music to bring the love of Jesus to the people of the Philippines. In Mindanao, Muslims commonly used cowardly terrorist bombings. A little while later, Steve's phone rang again with the same 007 international code. Trembling as he picked it up, Steve learned that his dad was gone. He had not survived the bombing. Later we would learn that Muslim terrorists had placed a bomb directly behind his father, while he had been standing in an airport waiting area, in Davao City. Not only was tragedy on Noit's side of the family, but now on Steve's side as well. Steve and Noit embraced for hours able only to cry. That was March 4, 2003, only four years since Steve and Noit had married. Now Steve's father was gone. Sadly, Steve's children would never know their grandfather.

Steve and Noit know that God still wants to use them in Cambodia. Their years have been difficult every step of the way. Literally, nothing has ever been easy, but they have been determined to never quit when pursuing what God told them to do. Steve and Noit still want to see transformation come to this nation, although on most days it is difficult to see any success. With all the tragedy they had seen in their lives it has been hard to imagine anything good. Will there ever be justice? How can there ever be restoration? Can there be true peace? Steve and Noit believed that God would restore everything in Noit's life, as the pastor had prophesied, but most days it was hard to imagine. They believed, by faith, that they would see it happen one day.

Part Three: Freedom Walk

For several years I had been thinking of a way to honor my wife, Noit. She survived the genocide of the Khmer Rouge, but just barely. Out of her once large family, only a small remnant would survive with her. When she was freed, life did not get much better. Cambodia was then occupied by the Vietnamese Army. Atrocities continued, but they were able to get a little more food to eat. The Vietnamese soldiers told Noit she could go home, but the only way to get home was to walk the 240km (150 miles) distance. She was freed during April, which is the hottest month in Cambodia. As soon as they were freed, they scavenged for food in places where they knew the Khmer Rouge had stockpiled food. They were able to get a few kilos of rice to help them on their journey home.

Noit's walk of 240km signifies to me the life Noit has lived. It was extremely difficult, and there was no one to help her. It was a miracle she didn't die. She had to overcome tremendous personal grief. Yet, she persevered and built a new life for herself. She came to faith in Jesus Christ and with the amazing grace she received, turned a life of insurmountable challenges into a life which would empower thousands of others to have opportunities and hope for the future in ways which she never had.

From Steve's Journal:

So why start the walk now, more than thirty years since my wife's walk?

It was April of 1979 that Noit was freed by the Vietnamese forces. Just like today, in 2013, when the temperature is 104 degrees Fahrenheit, (40 degrees Celsius), it was likely just as hot on those days as well. April marks the 34th year since she was freed from the Khmer Rouge.

Easter marks remembrance of the suffering of Christ. We mark the crucifixion of Jesus in every country of the world. It is a time of introspection and gratefulness for the suffering of Jesus, and in his resurrection, we are able to receive life! Easter, however, was unknown to my wife and illegal under the Khmer Rouge. The few Christians across the country had been massacred. During Easter season it is an excellent time to remember the suffering of my wife, and rejoice that our family has been forgiven our sins through the suffering and resurrection of Jesus.

March 29, 1975 was the date the Americans pulled the troops out of Vietnam in Operation "Frequent Wind". On April 12, 1975 the US military launched Operation "Eagle Pull" and the last US advisors and embassy staff evacuated Phnom Penh with their closest allies. In just a matter of weeks, all of Indo-China would fall to Communism. My father was drafted into the Vietnam War, so I heard stories of his time as a soldier my whole life. When I married my wife, it further linked my family's life with Indochina and the war.

April 17th marked the anniversary of the day when the Khmer Rouge captured Phnom Penh. That terrible time is marked with a holiday each year called the "Day of Hate" in which people remember the atrocities of the Khmer Rouge. They celebrate it in May marking the last major battle with the Khmer Rouge. While we do remember the atrocities of the Khmer Rouge, we live in forgiveness and help to minister healing to the people of Cambodia today. We do not hate.

My son Paul and I decided to set a goal of walking up to thirty kilometers per day, so that we could make it to the capital of Cambodia within ten days. We were not sure it was even possible to make this journey, but we were going to try. We would walk unsupported by any vehicles or additional supplies. We would not pre-plan our daily walk or schedule. During each day we would simply pray and ask God to lead us to people who would welcome us by giving us a place to sleep, or a place to rest, or to meet a new friend. We would re-walk the path that my wife took, though today it is a major highway and not the dirt track that it was when my wife walked it.

Walking a long distance, as far as a hundred miles, was not my first lengthy trek. When I was a Boy Scout growing up in the Philippines, each year all the troops would converge across from Corregidor Island in Manila Bay. It was a completely voluntary event, but I went many years in a row. During the start of World War II, General Douglas MacArthur was commander of the Pacific forces, which were based in the Philippines. On December 7, 1941, Japan initiated a surprise attack and bombed Pearl Harbor. At almost the same time, in another time zone, Japan also invaded the Philippines to destroy the American forces stationed there and occupy the country. The last holdout of the American forces was on a large rock island at the entrance to Manila Bay called Corregidor. It had been an important fortress to protect Manila Bay for more than 500 years. As the battle waged on and it seemed clear the Americans could not withstand the Japanese onslaught, General MacArthur escaped by submarine to Australia, proclaiming his famous words, "I shall return".

A few days after MacArthur's escape, the American and Filipino armies, under command of General Wainwright, surrendered to the Japanese. General Wainwright fought as long as humanly possibly, which infuriated the Japanese. It seemed impossible to dislodge the American forces from the rock island which not only had massive offensive capabilities, but extensive underground defenses. Eventually, with little food to sustain such a massive force, while the rest of the nation had succumbed to the Japanese onslaught, General Wainwright made the decision to try and save lives in the long run by surrendering. Even today, it is still the largest surrender of US forces in history. The Japanese forces gathered all the prisoners of war across from Corregidor Island and marching over sixty thousand men more than eighty miles to a prisoner of war camp. It included both American and Filipino forces. Many officers were executed. Along the way, if anyone became tired and attempted to rest they were shot. Anyone stumbling and tripping was shot. Anyone looking at a Japanese soldier was shot or bayoneted and left to die. Sometimes they executed the prisoners just for their own sick jokes. The result of this surrender was the loss of as many as ten thousand American and Philippine soldiers in what became known as the "Bataan Death March". It remains one of the most painful and humiliating losses in both American and Philippine history.

Each year, the American Boy Scouts would re-hike the Bataan Death March in commemoration of the loss and to remember again the sacrifices that these men paid for our freedom. Each year, the march would end at a giant cross erected on Mount Samat which was built in honor of those who died. On a clear day, with strong binoculars, you can see the cross from Manila, over thirty miles away. At the completion of the march, we would receive a commemorative medal at the base of the cross. I cherish these medals as much as my Eagle Scout medal because of its great meaning. I made my body suffer, although with all the comforts of modern hiking and camping gear. I wanted to honor the suffering of those who came before me, on whose efforts gave me part of the freedoms and comforts I have today.

I hiked the Bataan Death March three times and I hope one day I can hike it with my son so he too can know the suffering of those who fought for our freedoms.

But some say, why march? Why not just drive along and visit the cross in comfort? How many of you, before this reading, have ever heard of the Bataan Death March where thousands of American and Philippine soldiers were slaughtered in absolute brutality? Probably few, but because I have marched it myself, it is something I will never forget. I will never forget the sacrifices and suffering of those who fought for the Philippines in World War II.

Eventually, General MacArthur did return to the Philippines. When American forces liberated the POW camps, General Wainwright was saved, though his health was shattered and his body broken and emaciated. Though he was the highest ranking POW in American history (three star general), he was tortured and treated badly. The Bataan Death March, as well as years of torture in the Japanese POW camps, had played a heavy toll on his body, but he was alive. After Japan was bombed into submission, General MacArthur went to Tokyo Harbor to receive the letters of surrender of the Japanese forces. On the USS Missouri, General MacArthur stood and watched as he had a skinny and weak General Wainwright receive the unconditional surrender of the Japanese nation. Later he returned to the Philippines and received the Japanese surrender there as well. Unlike his confinement under the Japanese, Wainwright treated the Japanese soldiers with respect and dignity. Soon after, he was awarded the Medal of Honor, American's highest military honor, and his 4th star.

We must never forget the sacrifices made by the great men and women before us.

Though the Bataan Death March has great meaning in my life because I grew up in the Philippines, there was another march which was much dearer to my heart. It was the march that my wife made, not in defeat, but after surviving a genocide which claimed nearly her entire family. Weak and emaciated, my wife met the liberation army which told her she was free to go home after nearly four years in a captive hell. She marched to her freedom, a total of 240 kilometers (150 miles).

On the anniversary of her walk to freedom back in 1979, I walked with my son, Paul, to remember what she had lived through. We marched to remember and honor her. We marched to honor the victims, as many as three million at the hands of a brutal regime. We marched so that we never forget. We marched to honor the sacrifice of my wife and other victims of the Khmer Rouge genocide.

Today, for the start of our journey, Noit led me to the very spot where she was held during most of her time as an enslaved prisoner of the Khmer Rouge. Though the houses were gone and new ones built, the waterways were dried up and the stench of death was gone, she led us to the exact location where her little shelter stood. She had not been back to that place since she left in 1979. The villagers confirmed her amazing memory. I think with the horrors of those years it is impossible to forget. The village is just as poor today as it was during the Khmer Rouge, yet now people own the property.

Wherever my son and I walked today, the villagers were puzzled to see a foreigner walking. I told each inquisitive person the reason for my walk. This led to many amazing conversations. I told them that during the Khmer Rouge regime my wife was forced to work, and nearly everyone in her family died at the hands of the Khmer Rouge. When she was freed, she simply walked toward her home over 150 miles away. The journey took two months because her body was ravaged with malnutrition. Then I told them that I wanted my son to know what his mother had gone through. The reason we were walking is to honor my wife; my son's mother. People's initial response was almost always immediately, "What is her name?" This may not sound like a unique question to a westerner, but to an Asian it is rare that we speak of a person's name. Sometimes we may know a person for years yet never know their name. We speak to them with terms of respect like 'brother', 'sister' or 'uncle' and rarely use their personal name.

In response the people would often tell me their Khmer Rouge story. Most people I met were held in the same general area as my wife. I heard some shocking stories today, actually, not much different than my wife's, but horrible nonetheless. Most people I met lost their entire family. Then I realized why they were asking me what her name was. It is because they are looking for a connection. They are looking for someone to empathize with them. They are asking out of pain. They are just hoping that my wife would be one of their long-lost friends or relatives who they thought may have been killed during the Khmer Rouge. They are hoping that they just might be reunited with a long-lost villager who went through the same pain they did. Who starved like them; who lost like them; who saw unimaginable horrors like them.

So I would tell them, her name is 'Nimol', but her nickname is 'Noit'. Sometimes they would ask about their dead family members hoping they could at least add a piece of information to their memories. After one Aunty asked for her name, her response was, "Nimol is a beautiful name, I am sure she is a beautiful person too." Nimol means "perfect" or "without fault." Yes, indeed, Nimol is an amazing, beautiful woman. She has survived hell, and she now lives to love others with all her heart.

Walking hurts. People are often curious, but too polite to ask how much I weigh, so I break the ice and offer it to them. In February, two months before the walk, I weighed 412 pounds. Eeek! Then I began an exercise regimen and put myself on a special low-carb diet. When I started the walk I weighed 372 pounds. So, those twenty plus kilometers I walked on the first day really hurt. The most painful thing was carrying my backpack with my clothes, water and a little computer!

As I walked, we had neither a support vehicle nor plan of where to stop or where to sleep. My son and I just prayed that our journey would be led by God. This was a spiritual journey as much as a physical one. So, at different points I was honestly exhausted and prayed, asking God where to stop. I asked him to direct our path.

At one point during the day I started feeling wobbly, but the village market, where they likely had a place to rest and a cold drink was far in the distance. Suddenly, I saw a Foursquare church and orphanage. I ventured inside with my son, needing to just sit in the shade for a while. When I arrived I told them my name was Steve and I was a Christian too. I also knew their national leaders back in Phnom Penh, Ted and Sou. They were at complete ease asking my son and I to come sit under the fan.

As we talked, being noon, they asked if we had eaten yet. I told them we had not. So they said they would prepare food for us, but asked us to rest. They brought us cold tea and the children gathered around us. I took to singing praise and worship songs with the kids. We had a fun time. Later they brought their best food to us: some fish, mango salad and rice. It was delicious. Both Paul and I took a nap in the heat of the day. After our nap, they told us that most of the children were sick because it had rained a week earlier causing everyone to have colds and fever. We prayed together for healing. I was so touched by these little kids, some only eight or nine years old, but praying with all their heart. I'll admit I was moved to tears with these precious little kids. Though I could have paid them, they refused any money and I didn't want to steal their blessing as well. Since I knew their leaders and the orphanage, I could return to visit them anytime. While we were there, one of the older leaders was reading a book on her bed. When I saw it I smiled. It is called, "Keys to Preaching." Who wrote it? Steve Hyde! Me!

After it cooled off a bit, we headed further down the road, quite refreshed from our food and rest. We walked until my feet began hurting again. I told my son that we should pray that we meet a nice person with cold water, a chair and a fan. We didn't see anyone with a fan, but we found some cold water and a chair to sit on. I drank up several bottles of water very quickly. Then I told Paul that we would buy enough water to put in our "CamelPaks" which are bags of water in our backpacks attached to a hose and nozzle, making it easy to access the water without opening a bottle. We filled up our packs with 11 bottles, nearly an entire case of precious cold water.

While we were sitting, some of the same questions were asked, mainly, "Why were we walking?" After my explanation, a crowd formed and the owner of the shop shared with me about how the Khmer Rouge had devastated her family and now she only had two children left. As we were talking, a neighbor brought over a stand fan and blew it right on me. God provided a fan! Then I asked her how much my bill for all the water was as we prepared to leave. She replied, "Nothing." I insisted I had money and it was no problem to pay, but she said, "Please come back and see me another time and please bring your wife too. The water is my gift to you." My son was amazed at the blessing of God. This is unusual. Cambodians are a very giving people, but I am not poor to them. Often they view foreigners as cash cows, so this was unusual behavior. But that would not be the end of the generosity experienced.

As my son and I started off down the road, maybe twenty minutes away, one of the neighbors came racing along on a motorcycle and handed us two cold cans of coke and then returned home. We were so honored. Even though I didn't want to drink a sugar-packed soft drink, I knew that God was watching me, so he must have known that I needed some more energy! Once again we were amazed at the favor of God.

We continued walking. My legs were giving out. We had been walking since early in the morning and now it was approaching sun down. Our goal was to be led by God and we confidently knew God would provide our food and housing. The next village looked far, but we had no choice but to make it. In the village we found many unwelcoming people. They laughed at us. I felt uncomfortable, but I was in so much pain I didn't think I could make it to the next village, over three kilometers away. My feet were spent. I asked some of the villagers if there were any Christians in the village. Immediately, one partially-drunk man said, "Yes, that old lady down the road." I wanted to meet her. However, just as quickly as I started to move away, another villager said, "No, she died already. No one believes in Jesus here anymore." We continued walking. At the end of the village, I saw a man working at a small kitchen. I felt led to go speak with him. I asked if he had any food. He said, "No." Again, he was curious as to what we were doing, so I explained the story. After I finished, everything changed.

He said, "You wait here I will cook you a meal with pork." It was his own dinner. Then he asked where we planned to sleep. I said we didn't really have any idea. So, he said, "I am a policeman and I am going to sleep at the police post. I have water, electricity and a floor you can sleep on if you would like." I knew this was our man. Our man of peace. All day long I had been talking about Jesus, and tonight I am writing this from the police station. There were four policemen who have been so friendly with us. They offered us everything they had so we would be comfortable. We offered them Jesus.

That night we bid everyone "good night" from the village named, "*Snam Preah*" in *Pursat* province which means the "Fingerprint of God". All day, we had experienced the fingerprint of God. Thank you Jesus for always being with us!

Chapter ជំពូកទី ២២ 22

Sleeping at the police station our first night was tough. We slept on a hard concrete floor. They offered us two small pillows, so that was our only comfort. However, the location next to the main highway was the biggest problem. All night long, the sound of racing vehicles only twenty feet away from our room was nearly deafening. Sometimes the trucks would blow their air horns (just to anger the villagers, I assume). The police radio was turned on high volume so they could wake up if they heard anything important being shouted over the radio. Since I speak fluent Khmer, I was unimpressed with the police band. All night long, policemen in the area talked about a local concert, girls or what they would do the following day.

Then a horrible piercing sound blared out at 4am: monks started chanting on a megaphone! It sounded like they were in the next room! It was so loud! Then, BAM! All of a sudden I jumped up with extreme pain in my arm. I knew I had been bit or stung by something. I reached for my LED light and swatted at my pillow. It hurt bad. I woke Paul up so that whatever bit me would not bite him too. I swatted in the dim light at everything. Do you know what it was? A scorpion! I was stung twice, once on my hand and another on my forearm. Within minutes, my entire arm became numb from my shoulder down.

Day two of walking would be defined by the opposite of day one. Day two felt like the norm of my time in Cambodia. Most of my ministry life here in Cambodia has been just plain difficult. Nothing easy about it. Being stung by a scorpion at about four in the morning and then dealing with the swelling and pain in my arm all day long actually was quite routine for me. I know many would have been tempted to quit, or find a doctor, but I had been stung previously by scorpions. However, for me, there was no coincidence that the scorpion sting came at the same time as the monks were chanting. I prayed against the plans of the enemy and proceeded walking as we had intended.

The whole day was hard. Paul and I trudged up to 27km that day. We both had sore feet, legs, and backs. As it was getting dark, we were thinking of how we would get some dinner when a lady shouted at us from across a busy road. We carefully made our way to the other side of the highway. At first I didn't recognize her, but then I realized that I had spoken to this lady briefly at the entrance to a hospital a few hours back. That encounter, only seconds in length, opened something in her heart.

Immediately, she gave Paul and me some water and assured us, it was free. She asked why we were walking and what our plans were. I told her that I had already ditched our bags in the previous town and planned to go back at dark. She asked if she could fix us dinner. We were so grateful because we didn't have any dinner plans yet and it was already dark. By the next hour she had introduced us to her entire family and all her extended relatives. I shared with her about my walk to honor my wife and how I loved Jesus, who is the one who helps me to love others. She and all her family were interested to know more about Jesus. The meal she fixed Paul and me was one of the best I had had in days, if not weeks. It was delicious. In fact, it was my favorite Cambodian dish: *Snou Chrout Moan* (Sour Chicken Soup).

Thank you Jesus for helping us to be persistent and accomplishing your purposes for our lives. I thank you for the hearts you were opening at the same time that we were honoring Noit.

I agreed to do the *Freedom Walk* with my dad about a week ahead of time. I decided to go because we were going to do it in honor of my mom and of those survivors who did the walk as well. I was blessed not to be born during the Pol Pot era; and I'm more blessed to be born in the city during a time of progress, especially to be born to such a wonderful family: Mom, Dad, and my younger siblings: Anna, Odom, and Pearl. I am also very blessed to be properly nourished and to be receiving a good education. So when I hear about all those horrific stories about the Khmer Rouge era it makes me very thankful for everything I have. You have probably already heard or read about some of my Mom's stories and a lot sound quite difficult to believe. After my Mom was released in '79 she had to walk 240 km back to the capital when she was just skin and bones probably weighing only 20 kilograms (44 lbs) at the age of 16; I'm 13 and weigh about 60 kilograms (130 lbs), so it was extremely difficult for her. Yet she made it and is with us today.

Today the Pol Pot era has been over for some time and young people under thirty years old; mostly in the big cities, hardly believe or don't believe the stories their parents or grandparents tell them. Kids now have no idea of the unbelievable hardships their parents or grandparents lived through. I don't even know a fraction of these hardships. That's why my Dad wanted me to do the Freedom Walk with him, so that I may know a little bit of what my Mom went through during one stage of her life. The day before our big walk we left Poipet earlier than originally planned to be able to be closer to our starting point. On the first day of our walk we went to the exact spot where my Mom was held during the Khmer Rouge, after about 30 minutes of looking around and talking to the local families, my Dad and I started our walk. After about 2-3 hours our 20 kg (44 lbs) backpacks started to feel very heavy and our feet and backs started to hurt. We have met so many nice people so far on the road and they have been so generous. This is a big answer to prayer.

If I was in Mom's position 34 years ago, I don't think I would have made it apart from God's help. I am so thankful that God helped my Mom to finish the walk and get to a place of safety.

On the third day as I walked, prayed and listened to scriptures I was struck by my wife's walk, under a completely different situation than the walk that my son and I were taking. The hardest part about walking had been carrying the backpack with all our goods. I had packed very light. I had a few light snacks. I had a solar panel which charged my phone and computer as I walked. I had a portable water filter and only one change of clothes. The only "heavy" item was my laptop and the water I carried. I had about 6 liters of water at any given time.

When my wife walked, she had nothing. No shoes, no backpack, no food, no clothes and no water. Considering Noit's life, you would think her life began when we were married. She has no baby pictures. No pictures of her family members who were killed. She has no souvenirs from places her family visited while on vacation. She has no library of books. After Noit walked home from northern Cambodia, not even her home was left. Everything was destroyed and her family killed. She had, quite honestly, only a few simple pairs of tattered clothes. Even today, the only things Noit keeps that are of value are a few pieces of jewelry. She keeps these wrapped in a bag which she could flee with at any moment if required. It is the result of losing everything in your life. You value things differently.

When it comes down to it, I think there is only one thing that has value: LIFE.

I feel embarrassed for many news reporters who interview people in "difficult situations" (like the power went out for a few hours). Reporters use exaggerated terminology like "it is the end of the world" or it "looks like a nuclear bomb went off" which has no relation to the real situation. Some people think you can't live without electricity; some think it is impossible to live without McDonald's. We use adjectives which describe our situation as hopeless, yet it is far from that. Really, everything in our life is just temporal. We don't need McDonald's or even electricity. Would your life be difficult without them? Possibly, but you can adjust. So much around us in our life, some which we depend on, is actually of little value. The only real thing we have of value is our life.

Houses, jewelry, clothes, vehicles can all be replaced. Life, however, is sacred. As long as you are alive there is hope for the future. My wife stayed alive. Noit lived many years without hope, only wanting to numb the pain of her losses. Once Noit met Jesus she had new purpose in life. In Jesus, she is granted ETERNAL LIFE. Jesus promised her restoration of all things lost.

Jesus prayed to the Father during the Passion Week, "[2] *For you granted him authority over all people that he might give eternal life to all those you have given him.* [3] *Now this is eternal life: that they know you, the only true God, and Jesus Christ, whom you have sent.* [4] *I have brought you glory on earth by finishing the work you gave me to do*" (John 17:2-4). Jesus' desire was to bring Eternal Life to people. This is the same call God gave to us, as believers. This is the purpose for which Noit lives her life. Her life is of value when she shares the love of Jesus. Rarely a day goes by that Noit doesn't share, with complete strangers and friends, about how Jesus could change their lives.

As I walked down the long road, I found myself thinking about what has value. Nothing in my 20 kg (44 lbs) backpack had any significance for me. Yet I carried it to make my life convenient. Rather, simply the fact that I was alive was of the greatest value. The only question then is what will I do with my life?

Will I spend it filling my backpack with more things, or will I spend it helping the people I meet along the road to find life too: eternal life in Jesus.

On day four, we started off at a good pace, although a festering blister on my foot ended up getting the best of me. We were strolling down a newly paved section of road without a shoulder. The entire day's walk was in sand and gravel. It was like walking on a beach or in a sand box. My feet were being punished by the conditions. Just the day before, I had felt confident my son and I would be able to complete the *Freedom Walk*, but now it seemed impossible. As we walked, I prayed for God's grace and strength. In a small village called *Ansa Chombok,* we were greeted by a woman who offered to make us lunch and let us rest in her home. She even allowed us to take a shower in her bathroom and gave us a bar of soap to use. She was not a wealthy woman, but full of compassion. After four days, word of our walking in honor of Noit and the victims of the Khmer Rouge had preceded us. As we ate a wonderful meal prepared for us, two women shared their hearts with us. Many tears were shed as I shared about my wife's struggle. They shared their own stories as well. In a way, they vented their pain.

They told us graphic stories. I was torn whether I should let Paul hear such horrific details of cruelties done to these women. However, knowing that the same things happened to his mother, I wanted him to hear the firsthand stories so that he would know the truth.

The women described how they were ripped away from their families. Both, after surviving the Khmer Rouge, lost four or five children to sickness and starvation. Both of them were later divorced by their husbands who had multiple wives. They felt no love in their lives. They just wanted to talk.

One lady said, "When I walked, near Pursat province, I came into an open field which became known as '*Kabal*

Tahien' or 'soldier's heads'. I could not believe what I saw. Thousands, no tens of thousands, of heads were stuck onto bamboo poles around large pits which were full of bodies. The bodies were shriveled up, not swollen, because they were in the heat of the sun. The Khmer Rouge had called for a meeting of all able-bodied men, that they wanted to recruit to be Khmer Rouge soldiers. As they gathered them, in a large field, suddenly explosions started ripping bodies apart. The Khmer Rouge had intentionally lured them in to massacre them. After the soldiers blew them up, many were wounded but still alive, so the Khmer Rouge walked around and decapitated each one, putting their heads on stakes surrounding the bodies." She paused.

"These were my people who did this, Khmer. Not foreigners. These were my people. These were my people. How could they do that?"

Another lady added to her story. "Bodies were everywhere in those days. No one was honored. Even when my mother died hours after I last saw her I had begged the Khmer Rouge to let me go to her body. The Khmer Rouge leader screamed and cursed at me saying, 'What do you want with a corpse? You want to join her? If you cry, you can join her right now.'"

She continued, "You know, during that time many people died, not from starvation, but from celebrations. Once a year during harvest the Khmer Rouge gave us a lot of food to eat; as much as we wanted. This was only for a few weeks each year. Yet, during this time more people died than those who starved. The Khmer Rouge knew eating too much food would kill us as we were literally living on only a few grains of rice each day. They just laughed and let us have a party. After the party they would dump the bodies of thousands in nearby fields. We were nothing to them. We had no value. These were our people."

I know those images are horrible. These women were venting the pain that they have witnessed in their lives. I write them not to give you nightmares, but so these women can know someone cares about them, and will pray for them. Breaking with Cambodian culture, I asked for their names so you can pray for them by name: Om Heng (age 47) and Om Sarun (age 57). Cambodian's do not speak to people directly with their names, but use terms of endearment out of respect. I pray that somehow a great and merciful God will give them healing in their heart, healing in their lives, healing in their families and healing in their minds.

I now know the sound of nearly every kind of car, bus and truck in Cambodia having walked over 100 kilometers alongside one of the country's busiest roads. I know that any bus which comes within 4 feet of me is going to blow my hat off! I know when a car is passing from behind me how quickly I need to jump into the bushes. I know how to get my son's attention when I need to!

A funny thing happened as the two of us walked down the road. We had completed about 25 km (16 miles) each day so far of our *Freedom Walk*. We had been following one road all the way to Phnom Penh and were now over 100 km (63 miles) into our walk. There were no major turns or intersections to negotiate, though there were some minor bends and turns in the road. This morning, Paul was trudging along about ten feet ahead of me. Without realizing what he was doing, Paul kept his eyes down following a tire track in the dirt. The track gradually veered off the main road into some bushes and Paul continues following the primitive track. I shouted at him, but he didn't look up. He just kept walking. After about fifty feet into the bushes Paul looked up a bit perplexed, then he looked back at me standing next to the main road and just laughed. He was so focused on the next step, he forgot to look where it was going! He had just walked away from the road heading for the jungle.

Anyway, along the highway I can tell you exactly which cars are not a threat and which ones could potentially hit us along the road. Lexus 570's and Range Rovers are dangerous! The drivers of these vehicles are often young and seemed determined to kill people. You can hear the high whine of the engines as they race down the road at speeds of up to 180 kph (110 mph). And this is a narrow two lane road! At those speeds, they would kill anyone in their path and seemingly could care less. These are the cars of the elite of Cambodia. People drove by us all day long. It was a road that I had driven for years, but I never stopped and met people along the way.

Now traveling on foot, I met some amazing people and some people with deep difficulties. I met a man with no legs, waddling around on his torso. He lost his legs because of a landmine. He was gardening when I saw him! I can't imagine how hard life is for him. There is nothing handicap-accessible about a Cambodian village or rice field.

I met a lady who was completely broken. She was gathering something in a dry rice field. I snapped a picture of them right as God tugged at my heart.

My eyes noticed the boy sitting on the ground and I knew something was not right. I jumped off the road and into the field. The boy was sitting in a fire ants' nest. But why were they there in this desolate field?

I cleaned the fire ants off the boy whom I quickly discerned had a mental disability. He could not talk or function normally. There were no houses for quite a distance, but I saw a small grass shelter on the other side of the road. It was now late afternoon and the sun was going down. I knew what they were doing. They were digging for any insects or paddy crabs that they could find to eat for their dinner. This was their only food for the day. This was a broken family. These two kids and the mother were the entire family.

I sat for the next few minutes in that field with them and first explained to them about Jesus. They had never heard of Jesus in their whole life. I explained to them that Jesus loves everyone and that he can heal people because he is the greatest of all gods! I asked if I could pray for their son and explained what that meant. Paul moved in behind and put his hand on the young disabled boy. I knew that was a big step for Paul. The boy was filthy, and he could not communicate. The young boy just looked into my eyes as I told him, "Jesus loves you" over and over again in the Cambodian language. As I prayed I hoped for an instant miracle, but knew that my jumping off that road was a miracle for them already. How many American missionaries who love poor people do you find walking around rural roads in Cambodia at the very moment they were beside the road?

As we got up to go I reached into my secret stash of money and pulled out some bills giving them to the mother. Instantly she broke into tears right there in that dry rice paddy. She wiped her eyes as she clasped the money.

Paul later asked me, "Dad, how much did you give her?" I told him I honestly didn't know because I just reached in and gave her some bills without looking.

Paul said, "What if it was a $100.00?"

I assured Paul that the amount didn't matter, because God knew what she needed, and I knew there was enough there for her to eat well for some time. I explained to Paul that I don't have any of my own money anyway, it is all God's. I am only a steward.

Cars kept whizzing by. No one had any idea that God was at work right in the middle of that rice field.

There is a missionary in Mozambique, Africa named Heidi Baker who is one of my heroes. She has said many times that we believers need to "Go low, and go slow." By going low, she means we need to be more humble. By going slow, we need to really slow down and take time to love people. While walking through western Cambodia for a hundred kilometers, God has reinforced this to me each day; "Go low; Go slow." I see that this is a Biblical key which Jesus and the apostles modeled to us so we too can be successful in loving others.

I Skipped School for a Week

By Paul Hyde

I skipped school for a week. Here's what I learned:

Walking more than 150 km (93 miles) in the heat with 20 kg (44 lbs) on your back isn't easy, but possible. When my Dad and I walked we heard some pretty amazing and disturbing stories; usually both amazing and disturbing hand in hand. Even though those stories would scar most people just listening to them, it's very important that people don't forget about them. Those events are, both metaphorically and very literally, sin. It's disturbing to remember, but healthy to remember and understand in order that that sin doesn't repeat itself in the young adult generation, my generation, or any generation to come. My dad wrote a piece called "They Don't Believe Us" (in the next section) highlighting how some people in Cambodia don't believe the victim's accounts. I for one <u>do</u> believe them. Why? Well, you pretty much figure out that your parents or grandparents aren't lying when everyone over 40 in the entire country tells the exact same kinds of stories about horrific atrocities they endured. Not only that, but there is also a tremendous amount of proof all around Cambodia. The evidence can be found in every jungle, rice field, old school yards, Buddhist temples, etc. It's illogical not to believe. But don't get me wrong, even with all the proof I find it very hard to comprehend such disturbing history.

I never really knew much about my mom's history during the Khmer Rouge, only bits and pieces over the years. Only until pretty recently, I heard about where she was held, and how long she was held (officially people were released after 3 years 8 months 20 days. For some, including my mother, it was almost four years) and her walk to freedom with her mother, sister and little brother.

My Mom's mother and brother passed away before I got a chance to meet them. I'm very thankful that my mom and aunt survived the Khmer Rouge. I know that I have an incredible mom; she was strong enough to survive the Khmer Rouge and make that incredibly difficult walk back to freedom.

After this whole trip, if there's one thing I've learned it's that history is important as well as honoring people from history. That was the whole point of the *Freedom Walk* after all. I may have technically missed school but I really didn't miss out on my education. And I for sure want to do the *Freedom Walk* again someday, maybe with just my siblings and me (with dad giving moral support on a bike). After all is it even possible to honor someone too much?

Walking the *Freedom Walk*, by re-tracing the route that my wife walked on her journey to freedom from the genocide of the Khmer Rouge, has opened up so many emotions for my son and I which we could not have expected. While I have heard the stories of atrocities from my wife and others about the Khmer Rouge previously, re-walking a journey of over a hundred miles with my son, I heard victims of the Khmer Rouge say a shocking thing time and time again: *"They don't believe us."*

Sometimes they said it was their own children who didn't believe them. Other times they said it was just generally 'young people' who scoffed at them. The result has been keeping the past buried in their hearts. Deep scars of pain and loss still festering within them, further pronounced by the insensitive comments of young people saying, "I don't believe you."

I can think of nothing more painful or disrespectful to say to a victim of genocide. They deserve our honor and respect, not skepticism. Yet as I walked mile after mile and talked to survivor after survivor I heard it again and again. I heard it ten times, then twenty, then thirty, then forty. I realized that this was a common burden the victims are still bearing.

I determined that my son would never say such a hurtful statement. He has heard every story and more than I have written. I know you may be thinking it is horrible to make a 13-year-old boy listen to stories of horrendous atrocities committed by wicked people, but is it any less horrible for a boy to grow up and say to a survivor, "I don't believe you"?

So after a hundred miles of walking, I decided to make a random detour. In the village we happened to be in, I asked an old woman, who was also a victim, a simple question. Where did they massacre the people in this village? She said, "Go to Wat (temple) *Sadat Klok* and you will see." Being very tired, I asked a motorcycle taxi to take my son and me to the temple. Inside the temple grounds, only two kilometers off the main road I approached some young Buddhist monks. I asked them, "Excuse me, could you tell me where I can find the remains of the victims of the Khmer Rouge?"

The young monk scoffed, "There are none here, why don't you ask the old Abbott."

The Abbot said quietly, "Look in the broken stupa in the corner of the temple." (A stupa is something like a Buddhist mausoleum where the remains of family members are placed.)

I walked with my son toward a broken and dilapidated stupa, hats in our hands in respect for the dead. I didn't know what we were about to see, nor what my son would think of it. We saw many beautifully maintained stupas painted in gold. The families of rich people had made beautiful graves for the bones of their ancestors, but there in the corner of the temple was a broken and jungle covered stupa. There was a large opening on the top level of the stupa. I climbed up over vines and broken stones to get a clear vantage point. I peered inside and then called to my son to join me.

"Look Paul", I said to him.

There, in the darkness, were thousands of bones representing thousands of lives. Termites had been devouring the bones, but you could still clearly make out the massive pile of bones. The pile was several meters high and at least five meters square on the base. All human bones.

As we were staring into the darkness of the stupa, a young monk approached us and said, "There used to be more bones, but sometimes kids come and steal the bones to play with them, especially the skulls. If you want to find more bones, just look over in the trees." He motioned to a clump of trees about 100 meters away. "There are plenty more just laying around the ground over there," he said nonchalantly.

I told my son, "How can anyone say 'I don't believe you'?" Here is the evidence. In every village in Cambodia, every forest, every rice field, there is the evidence. Bones of victims dishonorably rotting away day by day and year by year." Most Buddhist temples and even schools were used as massacre sites. The Khmer Rouge wanted to specifically insult and desecrate religion and education by dumping bodies there. There have been more than 20,000 killing field sites identified in Cambodia, yet in reality, there is rarely a piece of land anywhere free of rotting corpses. Only one well known memorial, in all of Cambodia, has been erected as a western tourist attraction in the capital city.

Yet nearly four decades later, it seems few people care.

Just a week earlier, I had returned with Noit for the first time in 34 years to the site where nearly her entire family was killed and tortured to death. As a result of this walk, I determined in my heart that we needed to create some kind of memorial in that place. Surely, it is impossible to locate the remains of all the bodies of Noit's family, but she knows the precise spot where her life was forever altered. Let no one ever dishonor my wife and other victims of the Khmer Rouge anymore by saying, "I don't believe you."

Day 5 afternoon: Road Lined with Victims

As we walked down the road I seemed to be constantly talking with people, if not my son. I waved at every kid walking to school. I talked to teachers coming out of the schools. I greeted everyone on a bicycle. I said hello to people who watch their little stalls and sellers in markets. Pretty much the only people I didn't talk to were the people who whizzed by in those fancy Lexus or Range Rover SUV's. I am pretty sure that my son and I were tourist attractions there in western Cambodia. Everyone looked at us as they passed. I recounted my wife's story every time someone asked why we are walking. As I talked, a crowd always gathered. Sometimes we would sit and talk awhile. At other times I was able to have more private conversations. Everyone over forty is still terribly traumatized by the atrocities which took place under the Khmer Rouge and they readily told their stories of survival. Usually, our rest breaks along the road were tearful times.

On this day, I met a friendly lady. I didn't learn her name, but I politely called her "Aunty".

I was happy to meet 'Aunty', but I was sad at the same time. I could see she was still suffering from what the Khmer Rouge had done to her. Her life and her family had been decimated. She had no purpose or hope in life. Her entire family was killed by the Khmer Rouge. She was only slightly older than my wife, but looked more like my Iowan grandmother who was 101 years old at the time. She told me that she was beaten three times by the Khmer Rouge and left for dead. Her crime was that she was born in Takeo province. The Khmer Rouge leader in Takeo, "Ta Mok," was so ruthless that he alone was given the nickname, "The Butcher", out of thousands of murderers during that era. "The Butcher" made it his purpose to murder everyone in *Takeo* province. . . everyone. This little Aunty was one of the survivors, yet her body and mind had been broken.   She only weighed 29 kilos (about 60 pounds). Physically, she had never recovered. She said that sometimes she would go crazy and could not talk to anyone, but then after a few months, she would be ok. At that moment, she was ok. She was alive, but she suffered every day. She was alone. She had no one to care for her. No one to love her. Again, all I could do was cry.

All along my journey I have met countless victims of the Khmer Rouge. Their pains are still fresh in their minds. They still suffer their losses every day.   Some are physically or mentally scarred for life. I know that Jesus loves them and has the power to help them.   Honestly, apart from Jesus, there is little hope for the victims of the Khmer Rouge who still are hurting today.

I met two ladies who were held near the place my wife

was held. Their entire family was killed, except for a brother. They lost their mother, father, five more siblings, and all their aunts, uncles and cousins. Most they saw being killed or die of starvation making the memories even more unbearable.

I met another man who was a policeman. He said his legs were so swollen from starvation he nearly died. He described how where he was held they had only one cup of rice for 100 people. Soon the others all died. Still today he doesn't know how he survived. He warned me that we were walking through a poor area. Bad people might be tempted to rob me, he said, just because I was a foreigner and they knew I had money. He asked me to be careful. The Khmer people would never want to hurt a foreigner, but poverty makes the young people commit crimes. The policeman told me he would radio ahead to other police to watch out for me as we walked. I was grateful.

I met another woman who is what we call "Kampuchea Krom" as she was born in the Chao Doc province in Vietnam. She is ethnically Khmer, but born in what is today Southern Vietnam, which historically was a part of Cambodia. She was captured, along with other children in her village at about 5 or 6 years old, by the Khmer Rouge inside Vietnam. They forced the children to be soldiers and workers. She never saw any of her family again.

I met another woman who was the same age as my wife. She described everything she went through the same as my wife did, but she said she found a way to stay alive. Each night she was afraid the Khmer Rouge would come to kill her, so she would sleep next to dead bodies so that the Khmer Rouge would assume she was dead too. Nearly every night she slept with corpses. This was her strategy to stay alive.

I met a man who let us stay in his home that night. He was very small. He was taken by the Khmer Rouge and compelled to build water canals and plant rice fields. In April of 1979 when the Vietnamese Army invaded, he also walked back to his home, which was the same area we stayed in. When he arrived, there had been nothing left. The Khmer Rouge had destroyed the entire home. He only had a pair of black elastic pants, no shirt and no shoes. All of his family died. He shared that for the previous thirty-four years he had been trying to rebuild his shattered life. He admitted that he is still trying.

Walking the *Freedom Walk* was an emotional struggle as much as a physical one. I met beautiful people nearly every step of the way, but they were broken people. They were people who have been to hell. Yet, time and time again, I was told, "The young people don't believe what happened to us. They don't care." I told them that I cared and I promised to tell their stories too. Even now, the road to Phnom Penh is a path lined with victims of genocide.

Sunday, was a day of rest for my son and me. It was the sixth day of our Freedom Walk and a much needed break for our weary legs and bodies. Having walked nearly 150km (95 miles) already, our bodies were spent. Emotionally it had been a difficult journey for my son and me as we heard the stories of genocide and survival. Once arriving in *Kompong Chhnang*, a rest point for my wife in her journey as well in 1979, we spent the day ministering with a beloved pastor and long-time friend Pastor Houn.

Pastor Houn told me his story during the reign of the Khmer Rouge. He was a teenager when the Khmer Rouge swept into his village. He was separated into what is called the "*Kong Chlat*", or Teenager Unit, similar to the one Noit's older brother had worked in. These groups were worked hard and to death. The Khmer Rouge knew teenagers had more energy than most, so they utilized that to their fullest devious intentions. They used them to build massive water dikes, moving as much as 12 cubic meters of dirt a day by hand. They were not allowed to eat the spoonful of rice allotted to them if this was not completed each day. Houn, with only a third grade education, was a prime specimen for the Khmer Rouge's warped ideals: uneducated, hardworking and submissive. They worked him nearly to death. Each day, he thought, would be his last. They worked from the wee hours of the morning, all through the day, and were even forced to plant rice fields during the night by torch light.

Then one night at a community "building" meeting the community leader asked a question. (The community meetings were called '*Kosang*' which literally means "building up", but became synonymous with "execution". '*Kosang*' meetings were held nightly and the latest victims were taken away into the night and tortured to death for the sick pleasure of their captors.) The leader asked, "Who knows how to climb palm trees and tap their juice?" Two hands quickly shot up in the crowd. Instantly Houn had an idea. He raised his hand too. The community leader said, "Ok, you three, will now be responsible for tapping the sugar palms."

Houn had lied. He had never in his life climbed a sugar palm tree, or even knew how to. A sugar palm, looking similar to a coconut tree, can easily grow to a hundred feet high with no branches to cling on to. However, he had to hide his secret or it would mean death. He only knew that if he didn't get out of the Teenager Unit he would soon die anyway.

The next day the three were sent off to tap palm trees. He secretly watched each of the other men prepare as he fiddled with his small knife he was entrusted with. Soon, he learned how to climb the trees and get over his fear of heights. Amazingly, he was able to harvest more palm juice than either of the other two experienced tappers. From high above his perch he could see the workers below. He could hear their agony. Tree after tree he would climb, but he was given much freedom and no Khmer Rouge soldiers watched him as he worked. He was never fed any rice, but he survived by stealing drinks from the palm juice he was tapping. He dared not steal too much, but he continued to have the largest amounts of palm juice for processing.

Whenever Houn would see the Teenager Unit come nearby, he would climb down the tree, call the teenagers away from the prying eyes of the Khmer Rouge soldiers, and tell them to drink the palm juice as fast as they could. In this way, endangering his very life, he certainly allowed many others to live.

One day, Houn received word that his mother was sick and dying. He saw the Khmer Rouge unit commanders sitting around eating and drinking wine fermented from his palm juice. He approached them cautiously, bowing his head to petition them that he may have permission to go see his mother, as she was very sick.

Immediately, the Khmer Rouge commander pointed his finger down at him (this is a very aggressive and violent gesture in Cambodia) and cursed him by saying, "I will kill you, you #$%@ coward." Houn dropped prostrate to the ground fearing instant death. He raised his hands in humiliation (praying hands) over his head and begged for his life. The death blow did not come. He continued to beg as he crawled away in the dirt.

He didn't dare cry. Tears would surely be met with instant torture and death. The next day he climbed the palm trees again. He looked into the direction of where he thought his mother was. It was as if he could hear her crying from the tree. From his treetop perch he wept

uncontrollably. He never saw his mother again.

Crying from the treetops would become routine for Houn. He cried for his family, he cried for his friends and cried for his father who was also in some remote village. It was as if he could see the sorrows of the whole nation before him. He wept and wept from his isolated perch.

From the treetops he could also see the advancing Vietnamese army. Finally, in one day, it was over. He had survived. Only three of his siblings survived, but they were all glad to be alive. Soon the Vietnamese army was responsible for building a new nation. They looked for any medical personnel they could find. Once again, Houn volunteered as a medic. He didn't know the least bit of anything about medicine with his third grade education, but it didn't faze him a bit. Initially, they gave him a nine-month "refresher" course, which was his first-ever medical teaching. Within a year he was in charge of medical triage at a newly-formed hospital. He looked at everyone's wounds and decided which department to send them and learned basic first-aid. They were impressed with his efficiency and decided he should be 'upgraded' to a doctor. Soon, he was given a little more training and was giving hundreds of injections a day.

When I asked him how he could be so confident in his medical 'training', he just joked, "There were so many sick and dying people that there was nowhere to even step in the hospital grounds without stepping on a patient. I had to give hundreds and hundreds of injections per day. Anyone could learn medicine with that much practice!" Within a period of less than three years, including training and practical hands-on treatment, he was performing surgeries. Years after having retired as a 'doctor', many people still request the hospital to allow Dr. Houn to perform their required surgeries.

Houn is no longer a medical doctor. One day he heard

about Jesus and was given a Bible. He read it in the surgery ward. Other doctors would curse him trying to embarrass him. Very few people had ever met a Christian in those days. The Christian religion, as were all 'reactionary' religions, was banned by the communist Cambodian government. Medical staff in Cambodia could easily make money on the suffering of ignorant people in those days in Cambodia. They would routinely insist on irrelevant or fake surgeries in exchange for more money. They would force sick people to go home to sell their cows and homes in an effort to pay the doctors, before any medical service was performed. When Houn chose to follow Jesus his conscience wouldn't allow him to do those things anymore. He would help the poor people free of charge which angered the other doctors. The other doctors treated him terribly after that. Finally, he gave up his medical position in the government hospital to serve the Lord with his whole life. He later married. He and his wife together serve God with every ounce of their energy.

In *Kompong Chhang* province, where Houn was born and where he suffered under the Khmer Rouge, he now serves God and supervises the Methodist pastors for all of Western Cambodia. Nearly all of the more than twenty churches in the area were started by Houn and his wife. Every day, from the wee hours before dawn to late at night they serve Almighty God bringing restoration to their people. In the Methodist system, their salaries are determined by their theological education certifications. They were Christians long before the first Methodist ever touched Cambodian soil. They were starting and pastoring churches a decade before a Methodist Bible school was ever started. They survive, not on their measly salaries of two hundred dollars per month (which was determined by their lack of official theological training), but by selling off and renting every asset they have. They are servants of the Almighty God. Pastor Houn doesn't need a certificate to demonstrate his skills. He pours out love to others and he is respected nationwide for his pastoral heart.

When my son and I crossed the border into *Kompong Chhnang* province I immediately was drawn to walk to Pastor Houn's house. We walked and walked until we walked up to his church. There my friend stood ready to welcome two weary travelers and gave us a room to sleep in his church. My legs were so weak I had to brace myself to climb each stair to the third floor. Houn had built this room for guests so he could minister to them, not for himself. Instead, Pastor Houn and his wife live in a storage room on the side of the church which is barely larger than a small bed. The room he gave to us sits some thirty feet higher than anything around. It is a high perch. In the corner of the roof area is a single chair. It is Pastor Houn's chair. From there he sits, high above the town of *Kompong Chhnang*. He weeps for them. He intercedes for them. He sees their sorrows and he knows that Jesus is their answer.

Together Pastor Houn and his wife, much like my own wife Noit, have dedicated their lives to see Cambodia transformed by God's love. It is because of God's amazing grace that tens of thousands of lives, if not hundreds of thousands, are being lifted out of despair and hopelessness to a new life in Jesus.

Chapter 31

Paul and I awoke on the seventh day knowing we would complete the journey and arrive back at our home. Noit had been gone all week ministering to children in the slum town of *Poipet*, but would also be returning to Phnom Penh that day. Just as in the first part of Noit's journey, we wanted to repeat the journey she had gone through. In the town of *Kompong Chhnang*, just north of Phnom Penh, Noit had no strength to walk any further. She then traded her last asset, a cow, for a ride on a military truck to Phnom Penh. We also intended to take a truck to Phnom Penh. We didn't want to take a bus or a taxi, but some kind of truck that would be willing to take us for free so that we could experience a truck ride too.

We headed out to the main road looking for a ride. The normally busy road was now nearly deserted. It was odd. For the next half an hour we saw only private cars, not even a bus or a taxi. Then, about 50 meters away from us, a large truck stopped to buy a bottle of water. I quickly approached the truck driver and told him we were looking for a ride to Phnom Penh and asked if we could sit in the back of his truck. He thought it was strange for us to ask him for a ride, but he agreed. So, Paul and I climbed over the high sides of the truck, which was loaded with sacks of rice, and headed back to Phnom Penh. It wasn't long before the traffic got heavier and the air more dusty. We were arriving at the outskirts of Phnom Penh. Just like Noit had done, we decided to get off there and walk from the outskirts, through the city, and to our house. It would be a distance of only six or seven miles.

As Paul and I were walking that last hour of our Freedom Walk through the city, we knew it would be an easy walk of only a few miles. After walking 150km on dirt and gravel, now walking on paved roads was easy. The only difficulty would be the heavy traffic in Phnom Penh. As we walked, I had only one objective to accomplish before arriving at my house and that was to buy flowers for my wife and her sister. They were the only two survivors of the Khmer Rouge from their family. I had something specific I wanted to buy for them which I had thought about along the way.

I wanted the flowers clustered in the shape of a heart, showing my love for Noit. I wanted fifty red flowers signifying those family members and immediate relatives who died during the Khmer Rouge. In the center of the red roses I wanted two yellow roses. The color yellow in Cambodia signifies royalty. My wife and her sister are royalty and loved by God. Though my wife became a Christian about twenty years earlier, it was only a few years ago that her sister, Than, also believed in Jesus. Two pink roses would represent their mother, who passed away soon after they returned to Phnom Penh, and their little brother, who also survived the Khmer Rouge but died in

Poland. It was overwhelming to look at the size of the bouquet and to think about their loss.

Noit's brother, Sokhunthy or "Sit", was given a scholarship to study art, but the trauma (PTSD) of the Khmer Rouge stayed with him. In 1997 civil war again flared up in Cambodia, though briefly, and fearing the loss of his only two sisters, yet being unable to return home, he had a breakdown. He burned his passport and had to be taken to the hospital and put on medication. Soon thereafter his body was found. His death is a mystery. In fact, he too was a victim of the Khmer Rouge, but the trauma just took a few more years to kill him. Both Noit's mother and brother died as a result of the long-lasting terror of the Khmer Rouge.

That night I invited our close friends and family to our home. We fellowshipped and talked long into the night. Noit's family stayed the longest, sharing about their time under the Khmer Rouge and how they have coped since

those horrible days.   We then took a family picture. I think it is our first family picture.

My wife's family includes myself, Steve, and children Paul (13), Anna (7) and Odom (5).   Noit's sister Than's family include her husband Phal, also a survivor of the Khmer Rouge, and their three children Pin (31), Pich (29), and Own (24). Another son, Do, died in a horrific accident soon after Noit and I were married. This is the entire family. It represents restoration and building of a new family. With my American family, at reunions we often line up taking pictures with three and four generations.   With my Cambodian family, however, there are only two generations alive. Two whole generations have been decimated. This is the entire family which survived; only ten people including our children.

During the Khmer Rouge whole family lines were eliminated.   Even among Noit's cousins and distant relatives, whole family lines ceased.   The Khmer Rouge specifically targeted whole families.   Noit's family was a target.   They were labeled "17", a mark of death. Why? They were born in the city and had an education. That's it. This is all that remains, but our loving God can restore a stronger family which loves other people instead of seeking to destroy others.

Part Four: Restoration

Freedom Walk

Those who kill are guilty of murder. Those who killed a whole generation of Cambodians are guilty of genocide. Yet in the more than four decades since the Khmer Rouge took over and butchered a whole nation, only three people (of which only two were senior leaders), were ever tried for their crimes.

Our ministry in Cambodia, called Words of Life Ministries, is well known as we have been working with the Christian Church here for more than two decades. Because of that we often have random people showing up and asking for jobs. One day, a handicapped man (born with no forearms thus having stunted arms) came to our office enquiring about a potential job. He shared he was a Christian from *Kompot* province. My wife happened to be in the office on that day and met the man, in his late thirties. Immediately Noit's countenance changed meeting the man. After a brief chat, my wife said that she knew exactly who he was and knew his real name, "Agnong".

Noit and Agnong chatted a bit and then he left, never returning to our office again. I asked my wife who he was. She replied, that because of his unique handicap she recognized him immediately. His father was the leader of the Khmer Rouge in *Bakan* district who was directly responsible for the death of her family.

Noit's sister had helped care for Agnong as a child during the Khmer Rouge time. As she was dying of starvation, she crawled to Agnong's father who was the Khmer Rouge commander, and prostrating herself begged for food so that she would not die. Reluctantly, the commander gave a handful of rice to Noit's sister. It was too late though, her body could no longer take food and she died within a few days.

Agnong was too young to remember Noit's sister and she didn't bring it up to him out of politeness. Noit had no animosity toward him and was thrilled that he had come to faith in Jesus Christ. However, the darkness and guilt of the past was clearly too much for him to bear as he was trying to live in obscurity by changing his name and hiding his family associations.

These kinds of meetings are actually quite common in Cambodia. Those who committed the atrocities of genocide still live around us, and many even prosper today, while victims of the Khmer Rouge often have permanent psychological trauma which prevents them from living a successful life. There has never been justice for the victims of the Khmer Rouge. Never.

In addition to those who committed the atrocities against the people of Cambodia, there are plenty of accomplices. Politically, one accomplice which is frequently mentioned by the communist-leaning government is the United States. It was the US that backed a rogue general to overthrow King Sihanouk which led to the rise of the Khmer Rouge. The King himself even recruited young Khmer men to fight on his behalf in the Khmer Rouge. Our current Prime Minister was one of those recruited at that time. Then US carpet bombing with B-52 bombers, supposedly attacking only Vietnamese supply lines, created a bitter resentment among the Cambodians whose homes, livelihood and security were threatened by the indiscriminate bombing. There is nothing precise about carpet-bombing when one B -52 can drop more than a hundred heavy munitions to decimate vast areas of land at one time. As many as 100,000 Cambodians were killed in the bombings, which set in motion the Khmer Rouge coming to power. Even into the 1980's and 1990's, the US used its veto power in the UN to keep the Khmer Rouge on the UN seat for Cambodia. They did this because the Cambodian government was established by Vietnamese occupation forces. The policy of the US government was to block anything Vietnamese, because they were still reeling from the bitter memory of the Vietnam War.

The Khmer Rouge themselves were backed by the Chinese government. The Khmer Rouge leaders had direct contact with Mao Zedong (which is usually written Mao Tse Tong in Cambodia) and were implementing their own version of the Cultural Revolution in Cambodia. Millions of people died as a result of Mao Zedong's policies in China and the results would be no less horrendous in Cambodia. It is estimated that between 30% and 40% of the Cambodia population died through their "Maoist" policies. Noit recalled that the only foreigners she ever saw during the Khmer Rouge regime were members of the Chinese Army. In fact, there is still an uncompleted Chinese military base in Cambodia which was being constructed at the time of the Vietnamese invasion in 1979. The base is located in *Kompong Chhnang* province and includes a runway and mountain caves. It is likely that in 1978 and 1979 when work was being done on the base that China was going to use it to invade Vietnam. On December 2, 1978 Vietnam invaded Cambodia *enmasse* in a likely strategy to preempt the completion of the Chinese base. The Chinese responded in early 1979 by attacking Northern Vietnam. Both sides faced massive casualties in a war which has been lost to history. Because Mao Zedong and later Deng Xiaoping backed the Khmer Rouge and taught them to follow the ideals of the Cultural Revolution, millions of Cambodians died. Yet, no court would ever entertain a suit, nor has the Chinese government ever admitted any responsibility for its direct involvement in genocide.

On the western border of Cambodia lies Cambodia's "cousin" nation of Thailand. They are often referred to as "cousins" because there are many cultural similarities between Cambodia and Thailand. Both nations practice

Theravada Buddhism. Thailand has adopted many Khmer royal words and both have forms of Pali, the ancient language of Buddhism, that is mixed into our language creating many linguistic similarities. We share an 800km (500 mile) border with Thailand. During 1979 and into the 1980's as people tried to flee the war between the Khmer Rouge and occupying Vietnamese forces, Cambodians fled mostly to Thailand. At first Thailand refused to allow the refugees to enter. In appalling cruelty, the Thai military even forced thousands of refugees off cliffs of the Dongrek Mountains into Khmer Rouge held areas laden with thousands of landmines. Thousands of Cambodians died as a direct result of Thailand's treatment of the refugees. Cambodians will not soon forget the atrocities committed during that time against those who were fleeing genocide. In later years, the Thai government even provided sanctuary for the Khmer Rouge. Senior Khmer Rouge leaders and soldiers freely moved in and out of Thailand to elude the Vietnamese and Cambodian government, keeping them from eliminating the Khmer Rouge once and for all. The result was a guerilla war that was prolonged until 1998 when Pol Pot finally died. Pol Pot's final stronghold was only meters away from the Thai border where he had been furnished with supplies for years.

In 1998, for the sake of peace, the government agreed to a ceasefire with the Khmer Rouge and promised that no one would be tried for their crimes. Two new provinces were cut out from the Khmer Rouge strongholds and made into separate administrative areas with Khmer Rouge leaders still at the political helm. It was done for the sake of peace and a secession of hostilities. Those who were once Khmer Rouge leaders now live in fancy villas and drive expensive SUV's. Their children are often afforded the best education in the world, at schools in Singapore, the UK and even the United States. They have blood on their hands, but they live as the elite with complete impunity. None of the victims have forgotten the evil deeds of the Khmer Rouge in the past. The courts, however, are not impartial and will not entertain issues of the past genocide.

Injustice still abounds. Those who are guilty of genocide remain unpunished for their crimes and reparations never given. Murderers live among the population free from the fear of being brought to justice. Other nations, which were accomplices to the genocide, wash their hands and use their political power to be sure they never have to give account for their actions.

How does one heal in an environment of injustice? How does a victim contend with wicked people not only being free, but living in prosperity, seemingly oblivious of the tortured lives they left in their wake?

I believe only Jesus has a solution. Jesus taught us that in due time, God will avenge those who have been wronged. The Bible says, *"Do not take revenge, my dear friends, but leave room for God's wrath, for it is written: 'It is mine to avenge; I will repay,' says the Lord"* (Romans 12:19).

Some victims take heart in knowing that nothing will escape the eyes of God. Furthermore, those who seek healing in their own hearts proceed even to the most perplexing of Christ's teachings. The following verses say, *"On the contrary: 'If your enemy is hungry, feed him; if he is thirsty, give him something to drink. In doing this, you will heap burning coals on his head.' Do not be overcome by evil, but overcome evil with good"* (Romans 12:20-21).

Noit, and other survivors, will never see earthly justice in their lives for such horrific crimes against humanity. But Noit has chosen not to live as a "victim", wallowing in self-pity and bitterness. Instead, she has chosen to make a positive difference in her country. Through the model of Jesus' life and the empowerment of the Holy Spirit, she unconditionally loves the people of her nation so they can have a life which was never afforded her.

Chapter 33
ជំពូកទី ៣៣

In *Bakan* District in western Cambodia, where Noit's family was held and died, there is a sacred shrine that thousands of people give offerings to each day. The shrine represents one of the most significant spirit beings which Khmer people revere and worship. The name is "*Neak Taa Klang Meung*". It is an ancestral and territorial spirit.

The origins of this spirit are actually in a natural man who was a *kruu*. *Kruu* are a kind of shaman and spirit medium. Though *Klang Meung* was a regular citizen, not an official or military officer, he was a person who interacted with the spirits. The year was around 1500. During those days the Khmer Empire, which had once dominated the region, was in decline and Siam (present day Thailand) was surging. They invaded much of northern Cambodia, and most of *Pursat* province was also under their control. *Klang Meung* hated that his people and nation were in decline and put into servanthood under the Siamese army. Yet, he didn't see any way that Cambodia could defeat them.

Then the demons gave him an idea. There were thousands of wandering ghosts. While it seemed impossible that Thailand could be defeated in the physical realm, they were convinced that the Thai army could be defeated in the spiritual realm. Yet, *Klang Meung* could not accomplish this from using sorcery. He would have to become a ghost himself. He would then convince the wandering ghosts to cause the Thai soldiers to become sick and fearful. Then the Cambodians could defeat them in their weakness.

So, *Klang Meung* developed a plan to commit suicide along with his family and then go and then he would lead the ghost army to defeat Thailand. This was not a spontaneous decision, but a decision which was carefully calculated. He dug a large pit and planted spikes at the bottom. He made a small fence around the pit, which would be his grave. He then convinced his entire family, including his wife and brothers to join him in this suicidal venture. His wife was also seven months pregnant, thus her child would be killed as well. Amongst "*munakum*" (witchcraft rituals) he and his family approached the pit and one by one jumped to their deaths.

It is said that over the next few years, from 1510-1515 *Neak Ta Klang Meung* lead an army of ghosts to wage war on the Siamese army. He is worshiped today, especially by the military, for his courage. Even today, soldiers ask for his help in defeating the enemies of the Cambodians. He is a national hero and deity.

Historically, it is interesting to note that the Thai armies did not retreat until the French came to Indochina. In a land trade in 1907, the French gave parts of two other provinces to Thailand in exchange for the provinces of northwest Cambodia.

If there was ever a doubt that a spirit of death ruled Cambodia, this should be adequate evidence that the spirit of death is real. The ritual site of *Neak Taa Klang Meung* is in the very area where Noit was held during the Khmer

Rouge. Here, at the hands of Khmer people, hundreds of thousands of people were massacred. Death, indeed, reigned supreme in that place.

Today, however, there is another genocide taking place quietly across Cambodia and even the whole world. The genocide of abortion. It is interesting to see that *Klang Meung's* wife killed herself when she was seven months pregnant, thus killing her unborn child. In Cambodia each year as many as 60,000 or more babies are aborted. There are more abortion clinics in Cambodia than medical facilities which are able to fix a broken bone. Every district in the nation, and most villages, have access to inexpensive or free abortions.

The *Freedom Walk* to me, which goes directly through the territory of *Neak Taa Klang Meung,* is just as much a walk for life as it is a remembrance of the suffering of my wife. Everything my wife and I do, we do to bring life into this nation ravaged by death.

Jesus said, "*The thief comes only to steal and kill and destroy; I have come that they may have life, and have it to the full*" (John 10:10).

The Day of Hate and a Remarkable Witness

My wife Noit, along with all the other people who were living in the capital city of Phnom Penh, were considered worthless and expendable city people. The Khmer Rouge leadership had determined that all the nation's problems could be traced to the city people. They were viewed as oppressors because they were rich and they acted like it. Those wealthy people in the capital city knew they were a wealthy and educated elite and tended to treat the poor farmers badly. Therefore, the sinister Khmer Rouge leaders determined rather than to be executed, which would have been an easy punishment, and a waste of bullets and manpower, all city people would be put to work like animals. They would be worked to death. These people were called, "17". Noit was labeled "17". Her name, her life, her age and her identity were all irrelevant. To the Khmer Rouge she had no value because she was born in the capital city.

The number 17 comes from the day that the Khmer Rouge took over Phnom Penh: April 17, 1975. Since the defeat of the Khmer Rouge the country celebrates a national holiday called the "Day of Hate" on May 20. May 20 was chosen because it was the day when they routed the Khmer Rouge from the last of the cities in Cambodia. The actual holiday is officially called in Cambodian "*Tngie chong kumhung*" literally meaning "Day of Bitterness and Rage". It has been celebrated every year since 1979 when the Vietnamese and Cambodian forces beat the Khmer Rouge out of Phnom Penh. Those who celebrate it are those who were called "17" by the Khmer Rouge.

I don't believe that a person can move forward in emotional healing while still celebrating a day of "bitterness and rage". Remember the atrocities, absolutely; but continue to stir up bitterness and rage, no.

A few years ago, Cambodia's most unlikely witness of Christ gave a message of healing and forgiveness on national television. His name was "Duch". He was a Khmer Rouge officer who oversaw the torture and execution of more than 20,000 people. While still with the Khmer Rouge, fighting in the border regions along the western border with Thailand, Duch heard about Jesus. Someone gave him a Bible and he read it cover to cover. He accepted Christ and was going around spreading the good news of Jesus.

Once people knew who he was, he was quickly arrested. After a decade of detention, he was charged with "crimes against humanity" and "genocide". His trial lasted nearly two years. Actually, the court was limited to prosecute only the most senior members of the Khmer Rouge, but no one was talking except Duch, so they put him on the stand. He said repeatedly, "I should be prosecuted for the evils I have done in this world, but for me I know that whatever happens to my body, my soul is safe with Jesus." His very Christian witness on the stand each day often infuriated judges and victims of the Khmer Rouge. Many, not knowing what Christians believe, were puzzled by his confessions and his desire to seek forgiveness. No other Khmer Rouge leader has ever admitted to atrocities.

Finally, the trial was coming to a close. He had requested that his punishment be "death by stoning" so that he could die like the worst of sinners in the Bible. The court refused Duch had a chance to give his final defense and beg for his life. What resulted was the clearest presentation of the gospel I think Cambodia has ever heard. Mind you, the entire trial was broadcasted live on every television station in the nation.

Instead of begging for his life, Duch began speaking: "I know many of you wonder about my faith in Jesus and how that contradicts with my role in the Khmer Rouge. I want to talk about that."

Summarizing his twenty minute remarks about his religion he said, "I have studied Buddhism and was fully dedicated to following all the precepts, yet I found no peace in this. I studied Islam and read the Koran cover to cover, but I found nothing there to draw me. I was introduced to atheism under the communists and I strived as hard as I could to be the best communist I could be. Yet, I found nothing. Then one day I heard about the teachings of Jesus. I was given a Bible and I studied it thoroughly cover to cover. In the Bible the teaching of Jesus says to 'love your enemies' (Matthew 5:44). I knew that this was a radical teaching, unlike any other religion. I have studied all these religions and only Jesus teaches this. I appeal to my fellow Cambodians to believe in Jesus and follow his ways. Jesus is the answer for Cambodia. If we all believed in Jesus there would be no more wars, no more hatred between people and no revenge. I appeal to all of Cambodia to believe in Jesus."

Upon concluding his gospel presentation, the defense rested. Many in the court room scoffed; some looked puzzled; while others contemplated. His sentence was later passed down, ensuring he would spend the rest of his life in prison. Cambodians saw with their eyes and heard with their ears how Jesus changes lives. As Duch illustrated, forgiveness is the only way to bring healing to the land which still celebrates a "Day of Hate."

Many people have asked how a nation deals with the emotional and psychological trauma they experienced. How did Noit deal with it? The answer is simple. Jesus healed her heart when she forgave the Khmer Rouge.

How can a person heal from such atrocities? Let me just say that I have never been the victim of genocide, so I don't know. I have lived my entire life in countries marred by civil war, strife, killing and genocide. My father was blown up by Muslim terrorists. My wife's family were all executed, tortured and killed at the hands of the Khmer Rouge while she, a young girl from age 11 to nearly 16 years old, was their slave.

Being starved to the point of death causes pain. Watching people, including your very own loved ones, be killed causes distress. Being threatened that if you cry at the death of your loved ones, that your own life would be taken, causes intense fear. Seeing children being beaten to death and then eaten because of starvation, scars the mind in horrible ways. To be considered a "traitor" because you ate a single leaf, just to fend off starvation, damages the heart in horrible ways. Living in a prolonged state of fear sears the heart of anyone.

Walking 240 kilometers to a home, and a city, and a family, that has been completely destroyed causes unbelievable hopelessness. Knowing your family and friends were often killed by their own relatives, or those whom they knew, leads to distrust. Being a slave for an unknown cause, led by an unknown leader and being told repeatedly, "To let you live has no value, to kill you is no loss" reinforces a near permanent lack of self-worth. Even as a survivor, Noit had no hope in life. She only wanted to eat, work for money to buy food and sleep. Apart from that, she wanted to die because her life, as she saw it, was now worthless and there was no hope. She was an orphan who would forever be a victim.

How can a person who survived the Khmer Rouge possibly heal?

I am not an expert, but I would certainly say my wife has been successful in living a healed and restored life. From her example I would like to share with you what has been done in her heart. Noit has a beautiful heart.

After her freedom in April of 1979, life did not get much easier. 1979 was a critical year. Her mother had become so sick and weak during the Khmer Rouge she could hardly get out of bed. She soon died, without any access to medical care, leaving Noit, her sister, and her younger brother alone. Noit's sister, Than, married to avoid being forced to marry a soldier. This was a common "reward" to soldiers of any conquering army.

Than's husband, Prum Phal, had an equally difficult time during the Khmer Rouge, though he was not from the city. Phal's family was from *Svay Rieng* province located on the Vietnamese border. Because of its proximity to Vietnam, there has been significant inter-marriage between Cambodians and Vietnamese there. Vietnam was a direct enemy of the Khmer Rouge, so anyone who had married a Vietnamese was to be executed. Phal's older brother Sarun had married a Vietnamese lady before the war. When the Khmer Rouge came to their village they dumped Phal's brother, wife and their five children into a pit and executed them all together.

After the Khmer Rouge reign, Noit's brother-in-law Phal soon joined the newly formed police force and was able to secure police jobs for Noit and her sister, though they lied about Noit's age since she was only 16 or 17 years old at the time. Police were paid their salaries, not with money, but in rice. They would live. Yet, Noit had lost all hope in her orphaned life. She went to work for ten hours a day, then came home and slept, perhaps hoping never to wake up again. Phnom Penh and the whole of Cambodia had been completely destroyed. There was no water, no electricity, no food, no institutions, no schools, and no proper medical care. Pol Pot and his Khmer Rouge had decimated Cambodia and returned it to the Stone Age, which they proudly called "Year Zero". Living during those days was almost like being dead... and this was their freedom.

For ten years Noit worked. She was petrified by weapons, yet she was a police officer. She was impeccably honest, yet out of fear of being tortured for any infraction. She was extremely hard working; yet fearful the supplied rice would be stopped. She was extremely creative and resourceful because that is what kept her alive. Yet, her life was without hope. Noit was living as if someone had ripped out her heart.

After the Vietnamese withdrawal from Cambodia in the early 1990's when the Soviet Union collapsed (the Soviet Union was bankrolling the Vietnamese occupation of Cambodia), new things started to emerge in Cambodia. One was an English school called "Global Network" run by a returning refugee. A friend invited Noit to visit the

English class one day and the teacher talked about a strange God, Jesus. Though she had heard of Jesus, she had no idea about any part of the religion, much less anything about Jesus himself. A few years later, more foreigners came trickling into Cambodia. Noit's cousin had a foreigner renting a room at her house and invited Noit over to see this strange person. After time, this tall Dutch woman named Joke (pronounced "Yoka") was used of God to share the details of Jesus, and his teachings to Noit. Eventually, through God's providence, Noit came to know personally of Jesus and believed. Yet, her life did not change all at once. She still had little hope. She still lived in fear.

Noit remembers one day while she was praying she began crying. She didn't know what was happening, but she knew the Holy Spirit was working in her heart. She cried for hours and hours, and even turned into days. As she recalls, it was the first time she had cried since she was a young child before the Khmer Rouge reign. She had been threatened with her life by the Khmer Rouge if she cried for her deceased family, so she had buried her pain deep in her soul. In those hours Jesus healed her heart.

Not long after that, Noit prayed that God would give her a new job. She left the police force at the rank of Major. She joined with her missionary friend, now her adopted sister, Joke to start a project called *Hope for Cambodia's Children* under an organization called World Relief. For more than six years, Noit served as their co-director with Joke, helping tens of thousands of children to have better lives. Noit's life is a model of healing. Her life is one of purpose. From a life which could have been so scarred and permanently devastated, she has demonstrated unconditional love to tens of thousands of her people.

To bring healing requires more than remembering, but also honoring those who suffered. More than honoring those who suffered, it involves forgiveness from deep wounds within the soul; forgiving the killers who massacred one's family; forgiving those who made you suffer. Noit has done this in an amazing way. Half of the children she cares for today are actually the children of Khmer Rouge soldiers. Some of the lives she has poured her heart into were those who were involved in her suffering and her loss. This is true forgiveness.

Then, through forgiveness, God can restore all things lost. God is a God of restoration. Though her family cannot be brought back from the dead, her new family is far larger than she ever had. Her home is a gift from God beyond her dreams. God is the restorer of hope, of dreams and of lives. Noit lives her life today with a clear purpose and excitement to demonstrate love to her people. She exhausts herself daily so that children, hers and others', will not ever have to know the suffering she endured.

We live in a very broken world. Everyone has their wounds, tragedies and hopelessness. Yet, Noit's life is a testimony of how God can heal the most broken of lives. Put your hope and life in the embrace of Jesus and let him love you, as he did Noit. He will teach you how to forgive those who have hurt you so you can live a restored life.

Meeting with the Devil

Chapter **36**

ជំពូកទី ៣៦

In August 2014, the first senior leaders of the Khmer Rouge were convicted of "crimes against humanity"/ "genocide" some three decades after their crimes. The two old leaders, Khieu Samphan and Noun Chea, were given life sentences. In the last hundred years alone, some of the most evil people in history have walked the earth. They include: Adolf Hitler, who killed more than 12 million people, mostly Jews; Joseph Stalin, who is estimated to have killed at least 13 million people in the Soviet Gulags; Mao Zedong, one of the few whose government is still in firm control, is considered a national hero in China and was responsible for some 11 million deaths in his ethnic purge of the so called "cultural revolution" (though some estimates reach as high as 50 million people killed in China.) Japan in WWII executed some 5 million people. Cambodia had a horrible tyrant named Pol Pot who executed and starved to death some 3 million of his own people.

Cambodia, being a small country of 7 million people lost almost 40% of its total population. It is probably impossible for people to fully understand the horror for people, living in a country where every living person has lost some or all of their family, at the hands of evil men. Cambodia is one of the few cases in the world where genocide was carried out among the same ethnic people. Most other genocides are against minorities. The Khmer Rouge killed plenty of minorities too, such as the Kola people (now reportedly with only 31 remaining in the world), Cham, ethnic Chinese and Vietnamese to name a few. However, most that died were Khmer; from the very same ethnicity as Pol Pot himself.

I have often wondered, when watching an old documentary or war movie, what would I do if I had the chance to get near one of these evil men? Would I even dare to try to kill them? Wouldn't the world be better without them? Will they ever receive justice for what they have done?

Joseph Stalin
13 million

Pol Pot
3 million

Saddam Hussein
1.6 million

Kim Il Sung
1.6 million

Mao Zedong
11 million

Of the mass murders pictured above only one, Saddam Hussein, ever faced trial. The others were buried as heroes. They continued their oppressive control of others and genocide until they died of old age.

Nearly all of Noit's family were executed or died from starvation under the Khmer Rouge. Today, the biggest tourist attractions in Phnom Penh are the genocide museum and one of the 20,000 killing fields scattered around the country. The only complete census of the genocide revealed that more than 3,000,000 people died under the Khmer Rouge reign that lasted less than four years. (A UN committee gave an estimate of 1.7 million, which is often quoted. Later studies show that their methodology is prone to generalization and underestimation.)

I have often traveled into the Khmer Rouge areas today for the purpose of sharing the gospel. The head of Khmer Rouge propaganda became a Christian and has been broadcasting our daily Christian radio messages for three years for his comrades. Some 50,000 former Khmer Rouge soldiers can hear the daily Bible teaching broadcasts. It has taken since 1979 bring any of the Khmer Rouge leaders to trial. Pol Pot was the leader of the Khmer Rouge, but the Head of State of Democratic Kampuchea was one of Cambodian's most brilliant leaders, Khieu Samphan. His own doctoral dissertation written in France some 15 years previous to the Khmer Rouge rising to power described his extreme communist ideology and the need to purge society of all "city dwellers" and those influenced by the West. He took over full control of the Khmer Rouge in 1983 when Pol Pot became ill.

Over the years, working in remote jungle locations and mixing with former Khmer Rouge soldiers, I have often contemplated what I would do if I ever saw one of these senior leaders. Would it be a sin to hit them with my truck? Should I try to attack them with my bare hands? Would killing them bring justice to my wife, and her family, or the other 3 million who were killed? Of course I could never imagine meeting such a leader. . . It was all just day dreaming.

The answer to my pondering would come in October of 2005. I was in the former jungle stronghold of the Khmer Rouge, Pailin city. My wife and I were talking to the former Khmer Rouge Propaganda director when he mentioned the name of Khieu Samphan whom he had recently visited. Noit jumped quickly on the comment and asked if it would be possible to meet him. To our shock, he replied "No problem". The director called to set up the meeting for the next morning. I didn't sleep a bit that night. I thought of the irony of how other people get to shake the hand of the President of the United States or meet a celebrity or a very important person. But the most important person I had met would be the Head of State of the Khmer Rouge, who was responsible for killing 3 million people, including my wife's family. What would I do?

The next day came. I determined in my mind what course of action I would take. We suspected that in only a matter of weeks Khieu Samphan would be brought before an international tribunal to answer for the charge of "crimes against humanity". Yet, when we arrived at his home, there were no body guards, no fence, and no weapons in view. Khieu Samphan came into the room and sat right across from Noit and me, next to a friend of ours from America (Greg), as well as another of my staff members (who was also orphaned by the Khmer Rouge). At first it was hard to concentrate. I thought of the opportunity before me. This was an old man with no security. I could relieve the world of him with one hand. No problem. I contemplated my power to kill him and give "justice" to my wife and other victims. But, I also contemplated my power to bring him life.

He wanted to talk about politics, so we politely indulged him. He speaks English, French, Chinese and Khmer fluently. He was avoiding speaking in Khmer. Finally the door opened when he said, "My comrades are in despair in Cambodia." Greg quickly responded that Christians believe that Jesus can bring hope. He spoke in English but I wanted to speak to his heart so I spoke in Khmer, then Noit shared about how Jesus had lifted her out of hopelessness and into joy. For nearly an hour after the initial hour of politics, the man tried to get away from talking about Jesus. . . But he heard the gospel message of Jesus Christ more clearly than most will ever hear it.

He didn't accept Christ. He is a die-hard humanist. But who knows if a spark was lit? He invited us to visit him again later (if he was not in jail). In November of 2007 he was arrested by the UN and Cambodian Court called the ECCC. Only lawyers were allowed to speak with him since then. On August 7, 2014 he was convicted of genocide and given a life sentence. On that day, as was the day Pol Pot died, there was some closure for the victims. Yet, spending hundreds of millions of dollars to try three individuals seems to ring hollow in regards to true justice.

Noit, Khieu Samphan and Steve

Now I know what I would do if I met the likes of Adolf Hitler or any of these other devils. I would offer him life, not death. I really believe that Christ is the only answer for the world. Christ is the only answer for Khieu Samphan. As an old man he will soon face justice in eternity at the hands of the Almighty God.

Epilogue

When Steve wanted to go on this walk, I remembered the walk that I had made with my sister more than thirty years ago, and I didn't want him to do it. I knew it was a difficult journey and I thought since I already went through great difficulty, why should Steve and my son go through the same thing? When Steve insisted on walking I was already crying inside. Yet, somehow in my heart I knew that it was something God had led him to do.

On the day we were leaving, Steve wanted me to take him to the drop-off point. I didn't want to go, but somehow he convinced me to take him. I wanted only to take them into the general area, not to the very place I was held, which I have never been back to. However, as we approached the area with Steve driving, he drove to the very spot where I had been held as a slave of the Khmer Rouge. I had previously tried to visit the area, about ten years ago with Steve, but after getting off the main road and seeing one of the canal construction projects I had worked on my body went numb and started shaking. The memories were still too painful to bear. We left the area immediately. However, this time with Steve, we went right into the village where I had been held. I looked around for a moment to get my bearings. I told him it didn't look right, so please continue driving down the road slowly. I was looking for a certain bend in the creek and a tiny elevated hill. Then, less than 500 meters away I saw it. I told Steve to turn onto a small dirt track. As the trail ended, we were facing the exact spot where I had been held. We were on the very spot. I was not shaking. I was not crying. I was ok. I got out of the car and Steve and I started walking around the now empty field.

I knew immediately that my heart was different. It was healed. My memories of the Khmer Rouge are still there, but I have no pain in my heart. I have no paralysis, which had previously been present. After a brief stay on the land with Steve, he and Paul headed out walking down the dirt track. As they walked away I didn't want them to go, but I thought in my heart that God must have a special plan for them. So, I just let them go.

From there, I drove alone to *Poipet* in northwest Cambodia where I would spend the week teaching children in our Center there. Each day I prayed for them and my other two children who were still in school, back in the capital city, Phnom Penh.

Each day Steve called in the evenings and talked about who he met and the experiences he had. Steve talked about how everyone welcomed them and helped them. That put my mind at ease, because I was thinking about their safety. I had nothing in my heart that made me fear the walk they were on, or fear that anyone may try to hurt them. I felt at peace with it.

After five days of walking I received a call from Steve again telling me that they had arrived at *Kompong Chhnang* city. In my journey it took me two months to get there because I was too weak to walk and had no food. When Steve called me, I knew the hard journey was finished and I had great joy in my heart. At this moment I then thought about the love of God. I thought about how I didn't know how great or how deep is the love of God. I thought back to when I received Jesus. My friend had shared with me about Jesus telling me if I believed in Jesus, he could be my father. However, I didn't want that, nor understand it at the time. Then I thought about how much Steve loves me. That he would do such a thing for me just because of love. I again thought about the love of God and how recently, when I was praying, I had a vision of a deep ocean. In the vision, I was peering down into the

---

ocean and could see very deep down to the seaweed waving in the currents. Yet I heard God tell me, "No matter how deep the ocean is, my love for you is even deeper."

I asked God, "How deep is it?" There was no answer.

I knew that God loved me already. I knew it in my heart, but it was like I was still missing his love. Then when Steve walked, I felt Steve's deep love for me. At the same time I felt God's love for me too. At once it all came together and I felt the deep love of God, deeper than the oceans.

That night as I finished talking with Steve I immediately told all the children staying in our home about God's love and began to pray for them. The Holy Spirit moved and filled them with even more love that night too. Two girls were especially shaken by the love of God. That night I began to think of how I could thank my husband for showing his love to me, but it is hard to find the words. I now know the deep love of my husband and the deep love of my father God.

After completing the *Freedom Walk* honoring Noit, my wife and I have had many meaningful conversations together since then. Last night, as Noit and I talked about how Jesus had transformed our hearts and had grown His love in us, Noit commented on the condition of her heart immediately after the Khmer Rouge. Noit recounted:

Few people, probably, can understand what life under the Khmer Rouge did to a person's heart. Yes, there was the physical pain during the Khmer Rouge reign, as they worked us digging water canals by hand. They were miles long. The toil of planting and harvesting rice from before dawn and late into the night was excruciating. All of this was done on only a few grains of rice each day. With so little food, we lived at the physical limits of our strength and most people died because of this. Yet, the worst thing about the Khmer Rouge was the fear they burned into us. From moment to moment we didn't know when we would be killed as a traitor. If we ever stood out, either as weak or hard working, we would be killed. If we ever stole a leaf to eat, we had to confess for fear that someone saw us. We had to take the torture and beatings they gave us as punishment. We never knew who the Khmer Rouge were, who the spies were, or who could be a friend. In fact, there were no friends. We feared everyone. Everyone was alone. Fear was the worst pain in our heart.

Even walking back to Phnom Penh fear was everywhere. We feared the Vietnamese. We feared being raped. We feared they would abuse us and kill us. We didn't know why they were in our country and assumed they were there to imprison us as well. We feared ambushes and landmines. We feared death every

---

moment. Upon arriving in Phnom Penh the fear in us slowly deadened our hearts. As the new country under the Vietnamese occupation was formed, some normalcy returned, though fear was still present. The Vietnamese were not as brutal as the Khmer Rouge, but they still ruled by fear.

My sister was selected as a potential police officer and was sent to Vietnam for training. For three long months I was alone until she returned. She used her connections to get me a job the police as well. I worked from 1980 until the mid-1990s as a police officer. However, during this time, my heart had withered away until it was completely dead.

I don't know if you can imagine what a dead heart is like. Literally, my body felt nothing. I thought nothing. I was nothing. I only performed my duty like a machine. From the moment I completed my work I went home, ate some food, and laid down on my bed until it was time to go to work the next day. I thought of nothing. I dreamed of nothing. I had no ideas enter my mind. I did not think of pain. I did not think of the Khmer Rouge and my loss. I also did not think of happiness, nor what joyful emotions would be like. My heart was completely dead. The only thing I felt going in and out of my body was air.

This is what the Khmer Rouge did to me. They killed me. Only my heart had not stopped beating yet. They killed all our people. They killed my nation.

Then the Vietnamese withdrew from Cambodia. It was the early 1990's. Foreign troops came with blue helmets and lots of money poured into Cambodia. I continued to do my duty like a machine.

Then a miracle happened. I heard about Jesus. I didn't want this foreign religion nor did I want its rituals. I only wanted to feel again and I could feel Jesus. I believed. That was in 1994. Soon after I believed in

Christ I remember crying. It was the first time I could remember crying in my whole life. Under the Khmer Rouge if we cried, we would be killed. I cried for hours and could not stop. My heart came back to life when Jesus came in.

Recently, a missionary asked me, "Noit, you are so gentle and loving; so introverted, yet at the same time you can do anything. You engage with everyone and you have boldness to say or do anything to anyone. How is that possible?"

I just smiled and said, "Because Jesus healed my heart. My heart is alive and full of love. I have no fear at all. I have Jesus." The missionary probably had no idea how profound the comment was.

Noit is not a typical Cambodian and certainly not a typical Cambodian woman. She will love anyone. Man, woman, rich or poor, child or elderly. I remember when she hugged a young man dying from AIDS. His wounds were dripping with bodily fluids filled with the deadly disease. Yet, Noit showed no discomfort in holding him for hours as she prayed and ministered to him. He gave his life to Christ. He felt the love of Jesus through her.

I have seen her wipe the wounds of severely injured people or massage the legs of elderly who are unable to walk. I have seen her sit on the ground with handicapped beggars and clean the dirtiest children. She pours out her love, with no fear or restraint, on anyone she meets. She not only loves the poor, but she confidently shares Jesus with Khmer Rouge soldiers and leaders who directly murdered her family and friends. She helps them understand how God can fix their empty hearts. She knows what it is to have a dead heart. She knows what it is to be completely hopeless. She knows what it is like to not have any thoughts, only performing what is expected. I have seen her, without the slightest hesitation, share Jesus with senior government officials, governors, police and political leaders and wealthy tycoons. She is not intimidated by anyone.

Noit's very first act as a Christian was to tell her neighbors about Jesus and immediately started a church in her community which she still leads today. It is a church filled with broken people. It is a church of hearts that are still being mended. She pours out her life into others so they too may know what it is like to have a heart which is alive and filled with love.

Noit's life is an amazing testimony of how God can take a gentle woman and use her to bring healing to a nation. Through her life thousands and even tens of thousands of lives have been touched by the love of Jesus. Her heart is alive and what she lives for each day is clear: to love others.

The journey she has taken from the time the Khmer Rouge marched into her city until she escaped the clutches of the Khmer Rouge had been long and difficult, but the end of that journey led to complete freedom.

Freedom Walk Map

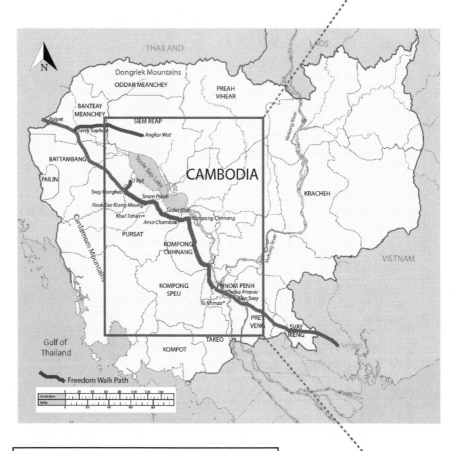

Legend:

PURSAT	Provincial Capital Names
O Bot	Village Names

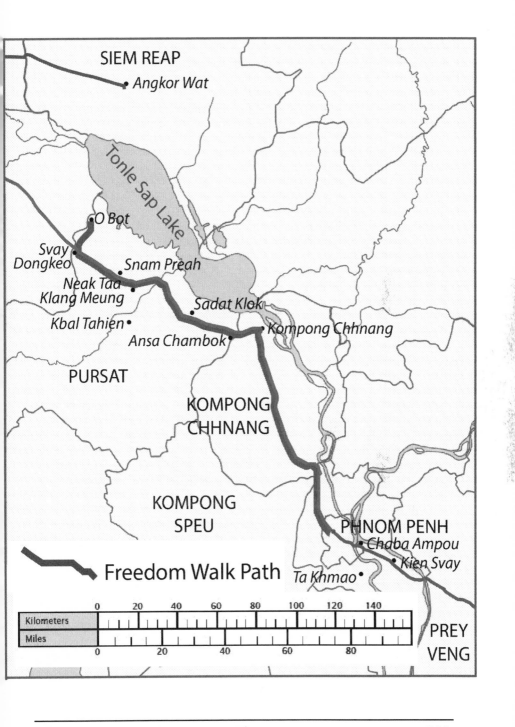

SIEM REAP
• Angkor Wat

Tonle Sap Lake

• O Bot

Svay
Dongkeo
Snam Preah
Neak Taa
Klang Meung
Sadat Klok
Kbal Tahien •
Ansa Chambok •
Kompong Chhnang

PURSAT

KOMPONG
CHHNANG

KOMPONG
SPEU

PHNOM PENH
• Chaba Ampou
• Kien Svay

━━━◣ Freedom Walk Path   Ta Khmao •

| | Kilometers | 0 | 20 | 40 | 60 | 80 | 100 | 120 | 140 |
| Miles | | 0 | | 20 | | 40 | | 60 | | 80 |

PREY
VENG

Achievements of Then Thuon Nimol
(Noit Hyde)

Before the Khmer Rouge in 1975 Noit studied until the 5th grade.

After the Khmer Rouge, at 18 years of age, she joined the Cambodian National Police as a Traffic Police Officer.

Working during the day and studying at night by 1990 Noit graduated from High School.

In 1994, upon believing in Jesus Christ she and a friend started the "True Way of Life Church" which remains an active community center church today in Chaba Ampou, Phnom Penh. Over the years she has remained the main leader of the church.

In 1994 Noit stepped down from the police in order to go into full-time ministry. She had achieved the rank of Major.

From 1995-2000 Noit co-directed World Relief's *Hope for Cambodia's Children* program which worked with more than 30,000 children by providing preventative health care, evangelism and community development.

Noit studied Theological Education by Extension and was one of the first women graduates of the program in 1998.

Noit married Steven John Hyde on March 6, 1999 in Phnom Penh.

December 15, 1999 Paul Steven Hyde was born.

Noit joined Words of Life Ministries in 2000 working alongside her husband Steve.

Noit received her Bachelor of Intercultural Studies in 2000 through Antioch Institute in Phnom Penh, Cambodia.

In 2003 Imparting Smiles Association Children's Center opened in *Kracheh* province with Steve and Noit as the founders.

June 10, 2005 Anna Nimol Hyde was born.

June 9, 2007 John Odom Hyde was born.

In 2010 Imparting Smiles Association Children's Center opened in *Poipet*, Banteay Meanchey province.

Noit received the "Royal Order of Moniseraphon" with the rank of Commander. The medal was from Prime Minister Hun Sen in 2010 for her work in helping children in Cambodia.

Noit received her Master of Ministry in 2010 from Covenant Theological Seminary in North Carolina, USA.

Antioch International School, Phnom Penh was opened in February 2011 in Phnom Penh.

In 2013 the Imparting Smiles University Dorm was opened in *Serey Sophoin*, Banteay Meanchey province.

June 12, 2013 Pearl Karona Hyde was born.

Hope Center, a women's empowerment center, was opened in *Poipet*, Banteay Meanchey Province in December 2014. Thousands of women are helped and hundreds of babies saved from abortion each year.

In March 2015 Noit and Steve received the "Servanthood" award from Bellevue Baptist Church in Memphis, Tennessee, USA.

Antioch International School, Reththy Number 5 Village, Preah Sihanouk Province was opened on December 5, 2015 with more than 100 students grades 1-6.

Noit became a naturalized US citizen on November 6, 2018 in Jackson, Tennessee.

Antioch International School, Poipet Cambodia was opened on September 1, 2019 and aims to be a K-12 school (Initial opening K-3).

Tens of thousands of people have been touched by the ministries led by Noit and Steve, with many thousands coming to Christ. Orphans cared for, broken women healed, lives of babies saved, and children educated so they can have opportunities to help their country in the future.

Lives Lost (Genealogy)

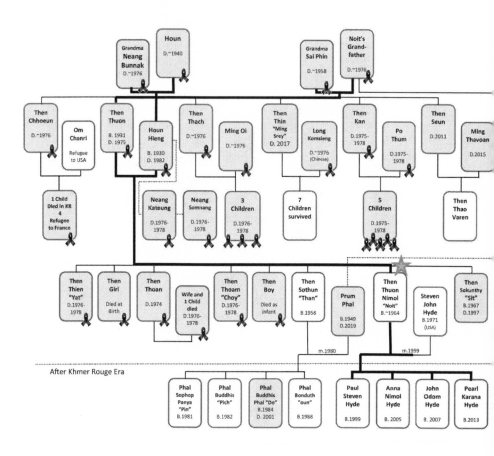

After Khmer Rouge Era

46 lives were lost from among Noit's immediate relatives as a direct result of the Khmer Rouge, either through murder, torture, starvation, overwork or lack of medical care. (Shaded names with ribbons are those who passed away.)

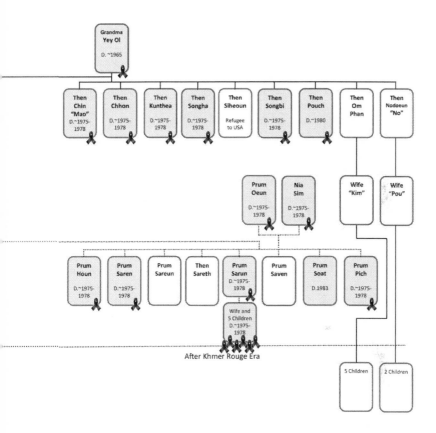

After Khmer Rouge Era

A normal family tree is called such because it takes the shape of a tree ▲. But Noit's family tree looks like a funnel ▼ because few survived the atrocities of the Khmer Rouge. This chart does not include many other more distant relatives such as those who had multiple wives, other cousins or more distant relatives. Nor does it include infants which died at birth during the Khmer Rouge, or children that were aborted.

Earliest Surviving Picture of Noit (1981)

Noit's Parents (only surviving pictures)

Noit in the Cambodian Police (1983-1993)

Our Wedding (1999)

Our Family (2019)

Imparting Smiles Children's Center (Kracheh)

Imparting Smiles Children's Center (Poipet)

Hope Center for Women (Poipet)

Antioch International School (Keo Phos)

Children's Camp

Steve, Noit and Paul at
the start of the Freedom Walk
at the exact spot where Noit was held
and her family died
during the Khmer Rouge genocide.

About the Artist

Moeun Chansokha, born October 12, 1957, is a self-taught Cambodian artist and Pastor of Freedom Church in Phnom Penh Cambodia.

Pastor Moeun Chansokha was born to his father, Moeun Saroeun, who was born in 1923 in Phnom Penh and his mother, Khim Saroeun, was born in 1928, also in Phnom Penh.

Sokha and his family were also victims of the Khmer Rouge. In 1975 when the Khmer Rouge took over they were a happy Phnom Penh family with 7 children, 5 brothers and 2 sisters with Sokha being the 3rd child. His grandfather, father, and oldest and youngest brothers died at the hands of the Khmer Rouge.

Sokha was forcibly married by the Khmer Rouge in a group wedding to Sam Samet in 1978 and they remain married to this day. Together they have three children daughter Sokha Ratha, born in 1981, a son, Sokha Visal, was born in 1986 and a daughter Sokha Sann Chan, was born in 1991.

Since 1979 he has held various jobs in publishing, accounting for government and private entities. He has enjoyed drawing and painting since he was six years old.

Since Pastor Sokha was also a victim and survivor of the Khmer Rouge he was able to draw the illustrations depicted in "Freedom Walk" as an eye-witness to the atrocities.

Steve and Noit live and work in Cambodia which is their home. Steve and Noit have been married since 1999 and lead Words of Life Ministries. In 2017 Steve was granted citizenship by the King of Cambodia for his years of service. They have four children of their own: Paul, Anna, Odom and Pearl. They also are Mom and Dad to hundreds of other children. Together they continue to love the people of Cambodia so that they can have a beautiful and peaceful future!